Coiled Designs for Gourd Art

Catherine Devine

4880 Lower Valley Road, Atglen, Pa 19310

Center Cover Photo: "Coiled Divine" by Marla Helton; Cover Page Photo: "Wound Up Tight" by Peggy Wiedemann

Other Schiffer Books on Related Subjects
Gourd Art Basics, 978-0-7643-2829-9, $14.95
Gourd Crafts, 978-0-7643-2825-1, $14.95
Left-Handed Stitchery, 0-88740-110-4, $9.95

Schiffer Books are available at special discounts for bulk purchases for sales promotions or premiums. Special editions, including personalized covers, corporate imprints, and excerpts can be created in large quantities for special needs. For more information contact the publisher:

Published by Schiffer Publishing Ltd.
4880 Lower Valley Road
Atglen, PA 19310
Phone: (610) 593-1777; Fax: (610) 593-2002
E-mail: Info@schifferbooks.com

For the largest selection of fine reference books on this and related subjects, please visit our web site at **www.schifferbooks.com**
We are always looking for people to write books on new and related subjects. If you have an idea for a book please contact us at the above address.

This book may be purchased from the publisher.
Include $5.00 for shipping.
Please try your bookstore first.
You may write for a free catalog.

In Europe, Schiffer books are distributed by
Bushwood Books
6 Marksbury Ave.
Kew Gardens
Surrey TW9 4JF England
Phone: 44 (0) 20 8392-8585; Fax: 44 (0) 20 8392-9876
E-mail: info@bushwoodbooks.co.uk
Website: www.bushwoodbooks.co.uk
Free postage in the U.K., Europe; air mail at cost.

Designed by RoS
Type set in Zurich BT

ISBN: 978-0-7643-3011-7
Printed in China

Contents

Dedication

In memory of my brother, who dared all, acknowledged his fear, and let it lead him into new adventures. This book is my attempt at overcoming my fears and moving on.

Acknowledgments

This book is the result of encouragement received from Darienne McAuley, whose hard work, experimentation, and years of teaching formed the foundation. She provided the structure and encouraged me in my work. Without her contribution of graphs and information, the book would be much shallower. Her research of Indian basket and blanket patterns forms the basis of the patterns, and her closed coiled gourds were the first and best representation of this skill that I have seen. I hope the book is a positive reflection of her influence. Additional thanks for the offer of chocolate at the end of my journey.

I'd like to add a special thanks to Jim Widess of the Caning Shop, in Berkeley California, for being the first gourd vendor that my husband and I met. He has been unfailingly supportive and encouraging over the years and has provided me with a steady supply of materials.

Of the many artists whose work I admire, only a few had photos available to include in my book. If I could have included all the works that deserve to be shown, the book would be too large to handle. My thanks for contributions from Barbara Bellchambers of Lakefield, Ontario, Canada; Leah Comerford of Falmouth, Virginia; Joanne Abreu of Albion, California; Peggy Wiedemann of Huntington Beach, California; Pamela Zimmerman of Beaufort County, North Carolina; Judy Wilson of Canton, Georgia; Stuart Fabe and Marla Helton of Greencastle, Indiana; and Wally Szyndler of Washington, DC.

A special thanks to Peg Arnoldussen for providing her pine needle stitch glossary and Lea Galcso from Pelham, Ontario, Canada for her assistance on some of the graphics for the stitches.

And, I am grateful to all the artists and artisans whose rich creations surround and encourage me.

Introduction

Coiling is a basketry technique used originally by indigenous peoples the world over to create and enhance the look of every day items such as storage pots, baskets, and jugs. They used whatever natural material was available for making the coils, including grass, pine needles, long bladed leaves, and bark strips. Porcupine quills, bone slivers and thorns were used as needles. Each core of material was wound tightly with thin strips of material that had been colored with plant and insect dyes, and they were stitched through each successive coil as it wound around. Making these items became an additional source of income and was developed to a high level of artistry over the years. An example of this is the work of the Wounaan and Emberá Indians from the Darién Rainforest of Panamá who, only within the last thirty years, began to impose onto their baskets colorful pictorial elements, such as birds, flowers, and animal designs. These baskets now sell for many thousands of dollars.

I use the technique for strictly decorative purposes and facilitate the work with prepared materials such as paper core and colored waxed linen threads available from basketry suppliers. This book is written for the beginner gourd artist as well as advanced enthusiasts who want an additional enhancement in their creations. I was encouraged to write it because of the lack of available material on coiling with waxed linen. I'm sure that it will save you time and frustration by giving you tips and tricks learned over several years of trial and error, both by me and by Darienne McAuley.

I've added a section on other coiling techniques, although I am not an expert on these. I rely on the contributions of other artists for this information. Hopefully, this book will help you add another dimension to your gourd art.

Simple examples of Darién Rainforest baskets. *From the collection of Alice Lyngard, Strathroy, Ontario, Canada.*

Chapter One:
Tools and Materials

Few tools are required to do the actual coiling, other than a tapestry needle. The main tools needed for any of these projects are used to prepare the gourd ahead of time. For this you need a saw to cut open the gourd, cleaning tools to remove the seeds and pulp, and a drill or awl for making the stitching holes. If you want to burn a design into the gourd, you will also need a burning tool. I am not going to discuss the merits of the various tools, since this information is readily available online or from any of the gourd tool suppliers listed in the back of the book.

The materials originally used by natives of Africa and the Americas were anything available in the area. Materials such as long grass, pine needles, palm inflorescence, leaves, or roots are still used as filler or core material today. For most of these fillers, you use a gauge to maintain a consistent thickness. You can make an inexpensive one from a one-inch section of plastic tubing, large straw, or copper tubing. You maintain the thickness of the core by adding material through the gauge as you coil.

For the projects in this book, we are using fiber rush, also known as paper core. This is brown paper twisted tightly and normally used for making chair seats. It is available from basketry or caning suppliers. Fiber rush comes in several thicknesses from 1/32" to 6/32". Rush that is 4, 5, or 6/32 inches works well for larger, thicker gourds. Rush that is 1 or 2/32 inches is known as baby rush, and works well for jewelry or small gourds. Thicker, colored rush is often called paper twist and can be found in craft and discount stores as well as basketry suppliers (see supplier list). I normally like to work with a 3/32" or 4/32" rush for regular patterns, but 6/32" rush if I'm only doing one row. This covers the cut edge better than the smaller rush.

Wrapping material needs to be strong enough to exert force and maintain pressure over time. Binding materials such as leather, cording, waxed linen, yarns, wool, twine, embroidery threads, and sinew can be used to wrap. Each material has its own good and bad points. Yarns, wools, and twine add texture and thickness, but eliminate detail. Embroidery thread is much finer and can add more details in the same space, but takes longer to wrap, and unwinds from the core material easily. Sinew and leather are natural looking and suit open coiling, but they are too flat and wide for closed coiling. Waxed linen is my personal choice because it is

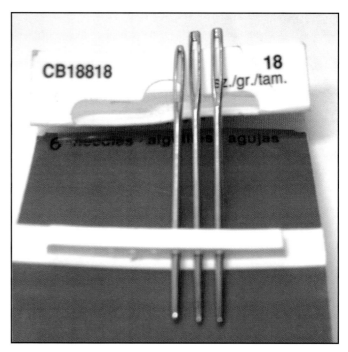

A tapestry needle has a large eye and a blunt tip to avoid tearing or fraying the core material, as well as the wrapping material. I use a number 18, 20 or 22-size tapestry needle. Size 22 is smaller and makes a smaller puncture between the cores, but I prefer the size 18 for easier threading and grasping. These are available at any store that sells sewing notions.

These are my personal tools. The different gourd saws and drills fit my hand well. You need a variety of scrapers to clean the inside of the gourd. The ball head is great for removing stubborn pulp. These tools are available at gourd suppliers listed in the back of the book.

Any firm cylindrical material works well as a gauge. Here I have a piece of a plastic straw; a piece of a pen casing; the bottom half of a needle syringe; a section of ½" copper tubing; and the empty core from waxed linen thread. Make sure the copper edges have been rounded off to avoid cutting yourself. Plastic tubing sold in pet stores comes in various sizes and is inexpensive as well.

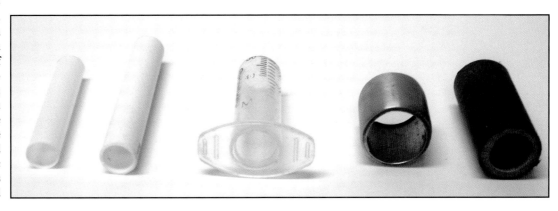

Various sizes of fiber rush, also known as paper core. Some even have wire centers to form shapes. They are available at basketry suppliers. Some hobby stores carry the larger diameter for floral arranging.

Royalwood Ltd.
517 Woodville Rd.   Mansfield, Ohio 44907   RoyalwoodLtd.com
1-800-526-1630   Fax: 1-888-526-1618

IRISH WAXED LINEN THREAD

Colors Available	2 ply	3 ply	4 ply	7 ply	12 ply
WHITE	x	x	x	x	
NATURAL	x	x	x	x	x
ROBIN EGG BLUE			x		
DENIM			x	x	
WILLIAMSBURG BLUE			x		
ROYAL BLUE	x	x	x	x	x
NAVY BLUE			x	x	
TEAL	x	x	x	x	
TURQUOISE	x	x	x	x	x
LAVENDER	x	x	x	x	
PLUM	x	x	x	x	x
SAGE	x	x	x		
MINT GREEN			x		
DARK EMERALD GREEN	x	x	x	x	x
DARK FOREST GREEN			x		
OLIVE DRAB	x	x	x	x	x
VICTORIAN ROSE			x	x	
LIGHT ROSE			x		
SALMON	x	x	x		
FUCHSIA			x	x	
COUNTRY RED	x	x	x	x	x
MAROON	x	x	x	x	x
ORANGE CRUSH			x		
LIGHT RUST			x	x	x
DARK RUST	x	x	x	x	
COUNTRY YELLOW					
BRIGHT AUTUMN YELLOW				x	x
BUTTERSCOTCH	x	x	x	x	x
WALNUT BROWN	x	x	x	x	x
DARK CHOCOLATE			x		
SLATE GREY	x	x	x	x	
CHARCOAL GREY			x		
BLACK	x	x	x	x	x

2 PLY   3 PLY   7 PLY   12 PLY

This color chart shows the thirty-three colors and five different thicknesses of waxed linen available. *Reproduced with the consent of Royalwood Ltd.*

strong, easy to work with, comes in several plies from 2 ply to 12 ply, and is available in thirty-three colors. It has the added benefit of being sticky, so that it holds on to itself and doesn't unwind from the core. Waxed linen comes in 100-yard spools and is quite expensive at around $10 each. However, one spool will coil nearly eight yards of 3/32" core, so it should do several projects. The dye lots vary widely from each batch, so order enough to do several projects. In our projects we are using 4-ply colored wax linen, or thread that has four strands twisted together. It is available at basketry suppliers and several gourd vendors (see suppliers list).

Work Safety

As a gourder, as well as a crafter, you will expose yourself to chemicals and sprays such as mineral spirits, spray paints, spray sealers, glue, and other products. In closed areas these can have a negative effect on your long-term health. Spend a little extra time and money and protect yourself, whatever craft you choose to do.

Gourds are plant materials that foster molds, both on the outside skin and in the pith inside. Also, gourd dust can be an irritant when inhaled. It leaves a bitter taste in the back of the nose and throat that lingers for hours and may cause hay fever-like symptoms in susceptible people. Because of this, I always advise my students to wear a mask when cleaning and sanding gourds.

If you are going to do many gourds, as we do, invest in a decent respirator, and work outdoors whenever possible. In Canada, working outside is only possible a few months of the year, so we have a studio set up in our basement, equipped with air cleaners, masks, goggles, and a shop vacuum.

When I'm working, I look like a mad scientist with my goggles, respirator, and lab coat. Being enclosed in my shower curtain cubicle with all the machines running heightens the image. Amusement aside, please take this health advice to heart if you are a serious gourder. I ignored the threat when traveling to a show a few years ago and made myself very ill. I had purchased gourds from a vendor in the south, and opened them without even a paper mask as protection. There was a mold inside that my immune system was obviously not used to breathing, and I developed a serious lung and nasal infection that lasted almost two weeks. Some investigation has been done on this problem and the experts liken it to a case of Farmer's Lung.

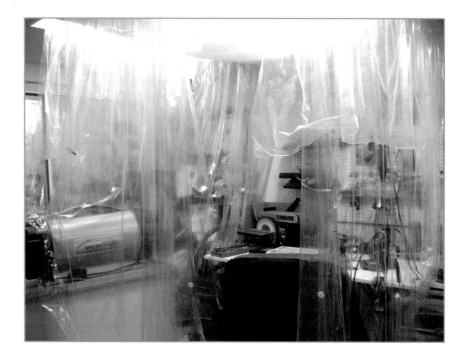

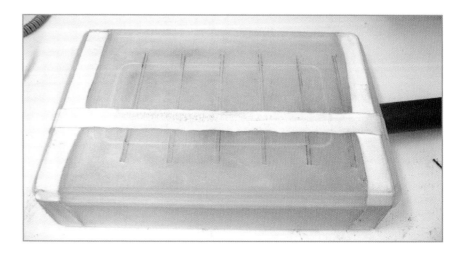

Chapter Two:

Getting Started

I preface these instructions by stating that I am a 'lefty.' I have written this book for right-handers, being that they are the majority, but I have included a section for the rest of us at the back. As all left-handers are aware, things don't work the same for us, so I have included tips for working with problems that right-handers never incur. This technique works well for 'lefties' with very little modification and can produce attractive patterns as well as provide great satisfaction. Check this section for hints before you start.

First of all, there is no right way to coil. This is entirely personal, based on being left or right-handed, a clockwise or counterclockwise worker, and so on. I'm showing you the way that I have found works best for the majority of people that I have taught. That doesn't mean it's the only way. If you find that my technique doesn't feel right after trying one project, then change the technique until it suits you. There is a section in the back that offer suggestions for left-handed people. Use this book as a springboard for your own creativity and discovery.

I'll be discussing two types of coiling; closed coiling and open coiling, with emphasis on closed coiling. Closed coiling is done with the core material completely covered by the wrapping material so that no core is visible. For this reason I use fiber rush for the core material instead of Danish cord, pine needles, or horse hair. Rush is cheaper and readily available. The design element is done through the use of colored threads and the position of each row of the coil. Closed coiling techniques will be covered in Chapters Two through Five.

Open coiling is done with a loose basting stitch that wraps around an exposed core. For this type of coiling, you want to see the core material so materials like pine needles, horsehair, or plant fibers work well. Various decorative stitching can be worked into the rows for added interest. These stitches work to strengthen the walls as well. Open coiling will be covered in *Chapter Six*. Danish cord will be discussed as well, but unlike the pine needles and horsehair, you don't pierce the core. The stitching process more closely resembles closed coiling, which is why I've included it in *Chapter Four, 'Projects.'*

Left: **I bought a portable air cleaner from Lee Valley (Canada) for under $50, and a respirator with replaceable canisters from Home Depot. There are many more models of masks and air cleaners on the market. Check the supplier list at the back or on the Internet if you are interested.**

Left: **I have hung several clear shower curtains to form a small cubicle that contains all our carving, sanding and burning equipment as well as the large air cleaner and the shop vacuum with lap attachment. The curtains are on rods so that they can be pushed back out of the way.**

Left: **I created a lap vacuum that my husband uses when doing his three-dimensional carving. I did this by cutting a round hole in the end of a large flat, airtight plastic container to insert the nozzle of the shop vacuum and then cut in several slashes along the lid for the dust to enter. It looks like an air register with a hose stuck in the end. It works surprisingly well for pulling in the fine dust that usually billows up and over my shower curtains. It has cut down on the dusting that I have to do after several hours of carving.**

Cutting and Marking

In order to make your coiling consistent and keep your patterns evenly spaced, the gourd needs to be divided into regular sections. Do this by setting the stitching holes in even, regular alignment. Keep the holes close to the cut edge of the gourd but far enough away so that the thread doesn't pull through the edge. The best distance is usually 3/16 of an inch below the cut rim. You can make it longer than that, but the stitches become a distraction if you get more than ½ of an inch. Use a compass to draw a parallel line down from the edge as a guide for the holes.

I use a marking technique developed by Ed and Darienne McAuley, and expanded by me for quick and easy leveling, cutting, and marking of the sewing holes. I use it for marking rim treatments on flat-topped bowls whether or not I'm working a pattern. This spoke pattern (provided in *Chapter Five*) is large enough to fit a medium-sized woman's fist. This is important for coiling, because you need to reach inside to pull the needle through. If you can't get your hand inside, you will need to use a pair of needle-nose pliers to reach inside. The spoke is also divided into twenty-four sections. Most geometric patterns are established by working from hole to hole, so having twenty-four evenly spaced holes allows you to make patterns based on 2, 3, 4, 6, 8, or 12 repetitions. There is more information on this in chapter five. The spoke pattern is there as well. Trace it or photocopy it whenever you need it.

On gourds with wavy edges or larger openings, I usually use my baby finger as a spacing guide between holes, or leave a space between ½" and ¾", adjusting the last three or four holes evenly to fit. If you want to be very precise, draw the parallel line down 3/16" from the cut edge and carefully measure the circumference (distance around). Divide this number by .50 for ½" spaces or .75 for ¾" spaces (pick the one you prefer for the space between the holes) to get the number of holes to place around the rim. If it works out to be an uneven number of holes that you can't divide into a repeating pattern, then adjust the size of the space until it works for you. Keep the spaces less than an inch wide; otherwise, the coil won't be firmly anchored to the gourd. It's better to have more holes, closer together than fewer holes too far apart.

When I'm not using the spoke pattern, no matter how carefully I measure and divide, my spaces never work out perfectly. I always end up adjusting the last few holes. You can minimize this problem by marking the last hole of each repetition, making sure that these sections are even, and then split each of these sections up into the number of holes you need for the pattern. Then if you have to adjust a hole, it will only be one hole in each repetition rather than three or four in a row.

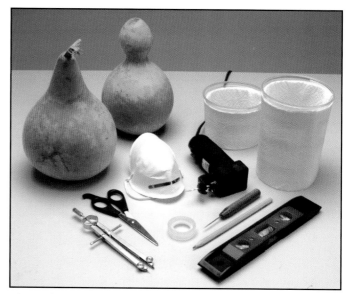

The tools required to cut a level top are a 3-way level, compass, pencil, short or tall plastic tub, awl, mask, saw, scissors and tape. You can create your own leveling tool by attaching a movable pencil holder to an upright rod.

Place an empty cottage cheese or margarine tub on top of the gourd. Place the level flat on the base of the tub and adjust the tub until the bubbles in all three windows are level. Hold the tub firmly and draw around the rim. You should have a level line to cut on. If the top is too tall for the tub, use a bigger container with the same size opening, or cut the gourd down first. Make sure that the bottom of the gourd is fairly flat so that it sits well and doesn't rock as you try to level it.

Cut off the top and sand the edge smooth and at the correct angle for your desired finished coil. I use a piece of sandpaper glued to a board to get the top even. The angle of the sanded gourd rim will provide the coiling with the desired slant; either a flat cut for straight sides; an inward slant for coils that narrow at the top; or an outward slant for coils that get wider as they go up. You can use a drum sander attachment on your drill to smooth the edge.

Use a compass set anywhere from 1/4 to 3/8 of an inch and scribe a line around the rim. This will keep your holes in a straight line around the rim.

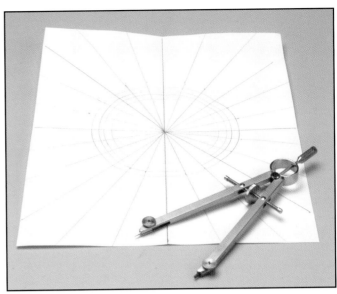

Copy the spoke pattern in Chapter Five, or draw your own circle divided into twenty-four equal spaces, as shown. The 24-spoke pattern works for an opening of 4 to 6 inches. After that, the spaces between holes become too great.

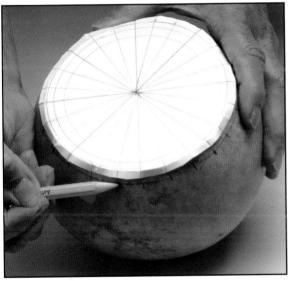

Center the trimmed spoke pattern over the opening and tape in several places. Fold the edge of the pattern down over the edge of the gourd and mark where the spokes meet the line you drew. Mark the holes with pencil to allow for adjustments.

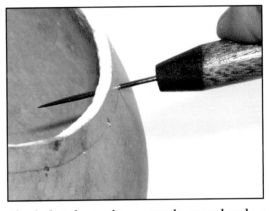

Check that the marks are evenly spaced and on the line you drew around the rim. Use an awl to puncture through the skin to guide the drill bit. Use a small drill bit 2/32" or 5/64" size to drill the holes. Sometimes, the gourd is soft enough to just push the holes through with an awl. Use an awl with a smaller shaft, since you only need the hole big enough for the tapestry needle to pass through. With thick gourds, make sure that the hole is at the same angle as the cut edge. Otherwise, the thread will be too close to the edge on the inside of the gourd and will rip through when you pull on it.

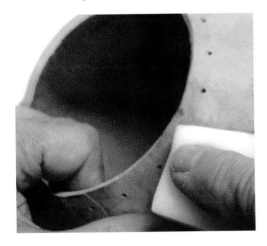

Use a magic erasing pad to wash away the pencil marks. These are available in cleaning supply sections of grocery or department stores. One brand name is Mr. Clean Magic Eraser®. (Do not use on your skin, as they are extremely abrasive.)

Finishing the Gourd

Coiling is the icing on the cake. That means that you need to have a completed gourd before you coil it. Any finish that you apply after the coiling will affect the color of the thread, or be affected by the wax in the thread. After several rows of coiling with waxed linen, there will be a light coating of wax over the gourd surface. This will repel or resist stains or paints that you want to apply. Waxed linen will absorb colors even though it is waxed. A benefit to that is that you can use leather dyes to change the color of your waxed linen. Be aware that some of the dye will rub off on your hands and clothing while working.

The inside of the gourd can be sanded and left plain, stained, painted, or decoupaged with paper or fabric using diluted white glue.

After marking and drilling the stitching holes, apply whatever design you want onto the raw gourd. You can burn, paint, silk dye, stain a pattern, or leave the natural pattern showing. Color the cut rim when you color your gourd because the edges will show beneath the coil. All water-based finishes must be allowed to dry at least overnight before sealing, to allow all the moisture to escape. I like to do the inside first, let it dry overnight, and then decorate the outside and let it dry another night. Doing both the inside and outside at the same time may trap moisture between the two layers and possibly result in a white film forming on the surface. If it is very humid in your area, let it dry longer.

Once both surfaces have dried well, seal your gourd in your preferred manner with at least three coats of sealer. Spray is quick and easy, but it takes at least three applications to equal one brush-on layer. Water-based sealers sold for decorative painting, or polyurethanes are easy to clean up, smell less and dry faster than mineral spirit-based sealers. If you are worried about using a water-based sealer over a water-based finish, then use a spray sealer or fixative first. I buy the same name brand spray as the varathane that I'm using to avoid mixing products. Always test the finish first before applying the sealer. I have ruined several hours of work by brushing on a water-based finish over a powdered pigment design that smeared badly. This is very discouraging, so take the few minutes required to test it. If in doubt, spray the sealer on first.

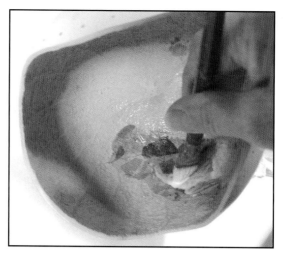

To decoupage the inside of the gourd, mix half water to half glue and use a large paint brush to paint the raw insides before applying the torn paper or fabric. This first layer of glue is necessary to help the material stick to the sponge-like insides. Add each piece and brush over it with additional glue mixture. Overlap pieces as you apply them. Apply as many layers of fabric, or paper as necessary to cover evenly and let dry at least 24 hours. If air pockets form, slash them open with an exacto blade, peel them back and add glue. Close the bubble up and cover with another piece of paper. Let dry again. Color the cut rim when you color your gourd because the edges will show beneath the coil. Seal the inside when dry using the same sealer as you use on the outside.

The constant rubbing of the thread over the gourd surface can wear off the finish so it's important to get at least three coats of sealer on before you coil. There are many brush-on water-based sealers, as well as sprays. Remember that you need several coats of spray-on finish to be as thick as the brush-on.

Once your coiling is completed, a coat of clear floor paste wax may be used over the entire gourd. The clear paste wax will not affect the waxed linen. Just be sure to buff well and use a blunt needle to clear excess wax from the rows of coiling. Paste wax can also be applied over water-based sealers. Do not use a liquid floor wax, as this is not the same thing as paste wax.

Chapter Three:
Learning the Basics

Starting the Core

Choose a paper core (described in *Chapter One: 'Tools and Materials'*) that fits the thickness of your gourd. If you are only doing one row, you need to cover the cut edge completely. If you use too thin a core, the edge of the gourd will be visible. A core measuring 5/32 of an inch or 6/32 of an inch works in most cases. These larger thicknesses are often available in color at craft stores and in smaller quantities. They are used in floral arrangements for ribbons or making paper flowers. If the gourd is really thick, then sand down the inside edge with a dremel-type tool until it is about half-an-inch thick.

You need to know before you start how many rows of coiling your finished gourd will be. You can cut off extra core, but it is really awkward to add a piece. To add, you need to angle cut the old and the new pieces, glue them together and hold them in place until they dry. The resulting thickness of the join is quite unsightly, and not as secure, so always cut more core than you think you will need. Sixteen inches is enough to do one row around the spoke pattern.

Placement of the start of your core is important, because no matter how carefully you coil, the place where row one rises (ramps up) to become row two will be obvious. This is especially noticeable if part of your design is directly above it. Also, your ending will be above the start, and because it is done as over-wrap anchor stitches for the last hole, it is noticeably different from the rest of the coils. For these reasons, place your start at the back of your gourd, if there is a front and back to your work.

Wrap the extra length of core in a loose circle, and secure with an elastic band. Leave enough loose so that you can sit on it or tuck it under your arm and still move the gourd freely. Pull the coil out, as you need it.

Place the core on the rim of the gourd to find the direction it wants to curl. It is best to work with the core, than to struggle against the memory of the curve. Cut the end on a sharp upward angle to make a ramp. Place the cut end of the core facing up and towards your right hand. The rest of the core is to your left.

Thread a tapestry needle on your chosen colored thread so that the tail is approximately four inches long. Stitch through the first hole once, from the inside of the gourd. Tie a double knot tightly over the paper core about an eighth of an inch behind the slant on the core. Pull the knot to the inside of the gourd, and place the tail end of the thread along the core, holding it in place with your left index finger.

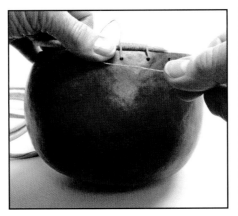

From the inside of the gourd, stitch through the same hole for a second time, pulling snugly. Hold the core in place and wrap the linen around the core using your right hand, by going over the top of the gourd and under your left thumb. Snug the stitch closely against the previous stitch. Continue wrapping until you reach the next hole. Stitch through the hole twice and continue wrapping until you reach the second last hole before the beginning of the coil. Make sure that each stitch is touching the stitch beside it and wraps tightly around the core. No core should be visible through the thread, and each stitch must be straight and uncrossed. Use your needle to straighten the stitches up if necessary.

Wrapping the Core

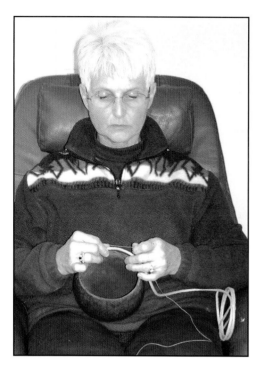

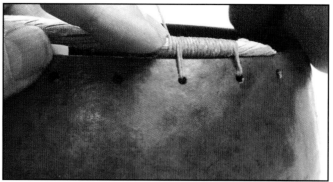

The right arm will move from the front of the gourd, towards your face, then over the top of the gourd, around the back and up under your left hand. You will release the fingers holding the gourd one at a time to pull the thread around to the start-ing position. You will quickly develop a rhythm of wrapping and releasing. Let the thread slide slowly through your right hand as you wind, and use the index finger of your left hand to push the stitches against each other. I sometimes wrap the additional threads around the baby finger of my non-working hand (left hand for you 'righties') to keep them tight and out of the way.

The most common way to work for right-hand-ed people is to sit with the gourd on your lap; the core tucked under your left arm, or left thigh, and working on the front of the gourd facing you with the end of the core pointing at your right hand. Sit in a chair that has low arms or no arms at all, to allow the threads to move freely.

How closely you pack the stitches depends on whether this is a single row of coiling or one of many. For a single row, you want the stitches packed as tightly as you can get them, without crossing over each other so that no core is visible. If this is one of many rows, leave a tiny bit of space between each stitch so that anchor stitches from the row above will slide between them. If you can slide a fingernail between the stitches, that is a good distance between stitches on an inside row.

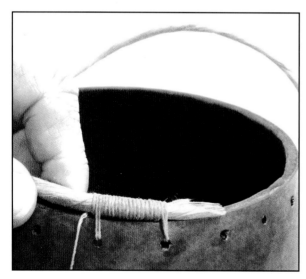

The main thing to remember is to keep your left thumb on the gourd surface (or the coil below) and your index and middle fingers on the inside surface. If you only hold the loose core material, the rows will not be close together and will not slant into the center in an even curve.

By applying pressure with the thumb of your left hand, you will make the coils slant in towards the center. This will make the opening smaller. Try to maintain a consistent angle on each row. It helps if the rim of the gourd is cut on an angle to start the first row slanting inward.

Adding Color

Adding additional colored threads to your work allows you to create designs and patterns, and helps you to tie the design of the top coils in with the design on the gourd. Choice of color is personal and sometimes unpredictable. You may like the colors you chose, but when you finish the design, it's not what you were expecting. To avoid this, I often work my patterns in color first on paper. It's better to spend twenty minutes coloring and discarding patterns than undoing three rows of coiling.

Working with color in coiling is similar to knitting. You carry all the colors along each row, and pull them out when you want to use them. The difference is that in coiling, you don't want to see them until you use them, so they are kept along the core material, and wrapped inside the coil. Also, you don't want any knots in your work, so you need to start the color well before you need it. Unless my design is solid colored for several rows, I start all the colors I'm using at the beginning of the coiling and carry them all the way to the end of the work. After you have done a couple of coiled gourds, you will get to know when you need to add the color, and when you can stop using it. It's common sense that if you are doing twelve rows of coiling and only using yellow in one spot on row six, that you are not going to start yellow at the beginning and keep it going until the end.

One of my patterns worked with seven colors wrapped inside the coil. It gets bulky, so it is necessary to keep all the extra threads on the back and bottom of the coil, and as straight as possible so they don't make lumps. The more colors you use, the more interesting it makes the design, but more care is required to do it neatly.

When working with different colored threads put a tapestry needle on each one. This saves time when you need to pull out a color to do a pattern or a figure "8" anchor stitch. Stopping to take a needle off one color to put it on another thread slows the work down. Tapestry needles come in packages of twenty-five from The Caning Shop, or packages of three from sewing stores.

Tie a single knot tightly over the paper core and pull the knot to the inside of the gourd. Place the tail end of the thread along the core and hold it in place. Take the other colored thread(s) and lay the unthreaded ends over the first stitch. Leave ¼" overlapping. From the inside of the gourd, stitch through the same hole for a second time, catching the added colored threads, and pulling snugly. Make sure that the added color(s) stay flat along the core and don't peek out between the wrapped stitches.

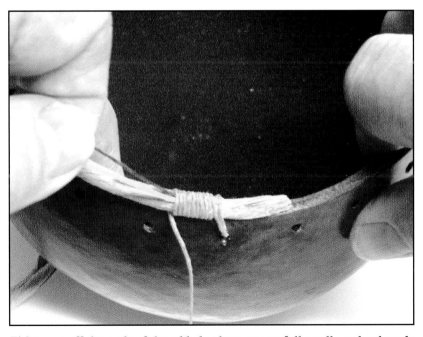

Either cut off the ends of the added colors, or carefully pull on the threads until the loose ends disappear behind the wrapped stitches. Do this slowly or the threads will pull out and you will have to go back and do it again.

To add more of the same colored thread when you run out, start the new thread when the old thread is about a foot long. Lay it along the core and wrap it in. Cut off the tail of the new thread or pull the new thread gently from the needle end to bury the tail. When you are almost out of the old thread, remove the needle and lay the end of the thread along the core. Pull out the new thread and begin wrapping, until the old thread is buried. Don't forget to anchor every five to seven stitches.

Eventually you will run out of working thread and need to add more. When you have only a foot of thread left, start a new thread by laying it over the core and wrapping it in. You need to have wrapped the new thread inside the coil for at least one hole before it is secure enough to use. Continue wrapping until there is only a couple of inches of the old thread left. Remove the needle, lay the old thread over the core, and begin wrapping with the new thread. Make sure you wrap in the same direction as before.

To bury the tails of added thread you can clip them close to the coil or gently pull on the thread until the tail disappears under the stitches. You have to do this within 8 to 10 stitches and pull the needle end very carefully or the thread will pull out, and you'll have to do it again.

Types of Stitches

There aren't a lot of stitches involved. You will be either wrapping or anchoring, and really there aren't many variations on the basic wrapping stitch. Either you coil left-handed, right-handed, towards you, or away from you. That's it.

There are a couple of things you can change about the anchor stitches. An anchor stitch is any stitch that holds the rows of coiling to the row below. The first type of anchor is an over-wrap or long stitch. This stitch is sewn around the row below as well as the top row, so it is longer than the basic wrap stitch. This is the stitch I use to start and finish the coiling. It can be used as a design element if you do it in a color other than the row below. It is very effective to start and stop a pattern, or you can do two long stitches on following rows just to one side of the over-wrap stitches below. This will form a slanted step pattern.

A lace stitch is an over-wrap or long stitch, but using the needle from behind and between the rows, you wrap a loop or two around the anchor stitch as it spans from one row to the other. This will separate the rows, instead of pulling them together, and make an airy, lacy look to the coils.

The figure 8, or Navajo stitch, is my favorite, because it holds the rows tightly together, and is almost invisible when pulled snugly. It is stitched from the front of the coil, under the row below, and back to the front between the two rows. This makes a loop around the top and bottom coil that looks like an eight. See the photos for details. If you are anchoring with a different color than the row below, you need to switch color just for that stitch, to make it invisible. This is a two-color figure 8.

You can anchor as often as you like, but the longer you wait, the bigger the gaps in the rows will be, and the less solid your coiling will feel. The native basket weavers anchor every stitch to give their baskets strength. Since strength isn't usually an issue in this type of coiling, anchoring every four to eight stitches works well. Because the two-color figure 8 is not as secure as the one-color figure 8, I try to anchor each time I change color, or after every four wraps with the coiling thread. This is a personal choice. You may only want to anchor every six or eight stitches.

Keep in mind that by anchoring your thread, you are adding an extra stitch to the row below. This can be beneficial if the threads below are too loosely spaced or the pattern is uneven. Anchor as many stitches as you need, in whatever color is needed to fill in the gaps. It can also be a problem if the threads are too closely packed, or your pattern is pleasantly balanced. Always think about where these stitches will be going, and how they can best work for you.

Experiment with the over-wrap (long stitch), one-color figure 8 (Navajo stitch), and two-color figure 8 stitches to see how they change the design.

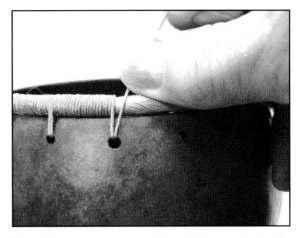

To make an over-wrap anchor stitch, on the beginning row of coiling, use the needle to sew the wrapping thread through the hole in the gourd rim. Do it twice for strength. I'm wrapping away from my body, so the needle will come from inside the gourd to the outside.

To make an over-wrap anchor stitch on a regular row of coiling, use the needle to separate the stitches directly below where the next stitch would be. This allows the new stitch to slide in and become part of the coil below. You want to keep the stitches straight up and down, and side by side. Stitch the needle from inside the gourd, under the row below and pull the thread tightly until it fits between the stitches.

The thread will wrap both rows of coiling. Only one anchor stitch is necessary on a regular anchor, but you may need two if you are forming free loops, or handles, or wish to make a design element. Pull the thread back between the two rows of core, and continue wrapping.

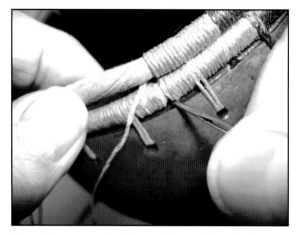

To make a one color figure eight anchor stitch, separate the stitches directly below and take the needle to the front of the row below. Stitch through and pull the thread tightly to slide between the other threads.

Bring the needle from inside the gourd, between the two coils and behind the anchor stitch. Pull hard to hide the stitch on the inside of the coil and to hold the coils together.

If you separate the two coils and look carefully, you will see an 'X' where the threads cross. If you could see without the core, the thread would make a figure 8.

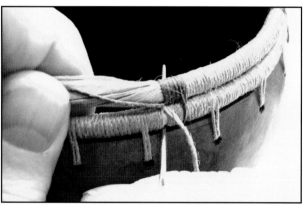

Sometimes you need to anchor, but the color on the row below is different from the one you are using. Separate the thread on the row below. Pull out the thread that matches the color below and stitch from the front, through between the coils and back behind the anchor thread (same as the regular figure 8). Place this thread back along the core and continue wrapping with your original color.

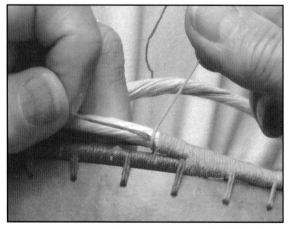

The bottom color thread will want to pull loose, so pull it tightly. Make sure that you wrap it inside the coil when you continue.

To create a lacy stitch, do an over-wrap stitch by bringing the thread up, over and underneath the row below, and using the needle between the two rows, wrap a loop or two around the anchor stitch as it spans from one row to the other. This will separate the rows, instead of pulling them together, and make an airy, lacy look to the coils.

Ramping

To continue the coiling on to another row, you need an incline that gradually leads the core up, so I call it the "ramp." If you cut your beginning angle too short, there will be a jump where the core rises over the ramp to become the second row. A good distance to make the ramp is the length between two holes.

After working with the core on the first row, it can twist out of position so when you get ready to go to the second row, your angle cut may be facing the wrong way. Try to trim it so that it still slants upward. This ramp is going to be wrapped inside the coiling of the core as you move to the second row, so you must sew between the last two holes. It will be bulkier in this spot, which is why I suggest that this be done on the back of the gourd, or in a place that isn't going to be the focus of attention.

When making a pattern, try not to have any part of the design directly over this ramp because the rows tilt here and any pattern above that will be on an angle. It's not always possible if you are doing a very complicated pattern, but keep it mind when starting out.

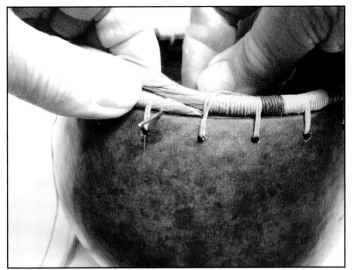

Make sure that the ramp on the beginning coil is still facing upward. As your stitches get close to touching the beginning core, use the needle to stitch under the core. Put the needle through at the farthest point possible and slide the thread into place until it catches the end of the ramp.

Hold the ramp firmly in place with your left thumb while you stitch because it will bulge out of position if you pull the threads too hard at the start. Wrap until you are directly above the first anchor stitch. From inside the gourd, stitch between the core and the edge, between the two anchor stitches. Wrap over the top and bring the thread out between the two rows of core. Begin wrapping on the second row. (It will be in the same place as the yellow thread showing in the photo.)

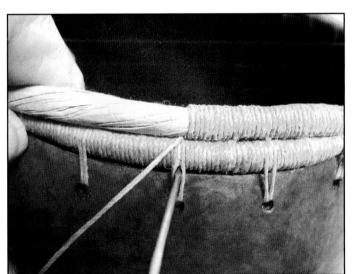

On the second row, the anchor points should be above each hole and the center of each space. This works out to be an anchor every five to seven stitches. To anchor above a hole, bring the needle from the front, below the core, and between the two anchor threads. Try to get between the threads at the back as well.

Changing Colors

As you coil, you will be carrying the extra colored threads along the core and wrapping them with the working thread. All these loose threads and core tend to get tangled, so make sure your workspace is open enough. Also, discourage your pets from chewing on the threads. Cats especially can swallow the thread with needles attached, as well as damage the threads by biting them.

You can wrap the excess core material in an elastic band, but since you're frequently using the threads, you can't wrap them up. Just remember to keep the extra threads along the core and the working thread on the opposite side. I often wrap the extra colored threads around my baby finger to keep them tight.

To change from one color to the other, place the working thread from your right hand over the core on your left side. Do this first. Now find the color that you want and pull it out to the front of your work, below the core and any other colored thread. The new color must always be below the others so that when you wrap, it covers them all. Try to keep the colors straight on the back of the core to avoid unsightly bumps in your work. Constantly check to make sure that the threads are all buried and flat.

When changing color, it often happens that you start wrapping in the opposite direction. This is because the new color is inside the gourd and you must bring it to the front between the cores. If you find you have done this, you can undo back to the color change, or just wait until you change colors again, and correct it. The direction of coiling won't be obvious by looking at the outside of your work.

To change the working color, lay it along the back of the core on the opposite side. Do this first, before pulling out the new color. I like to anchor before each color change.

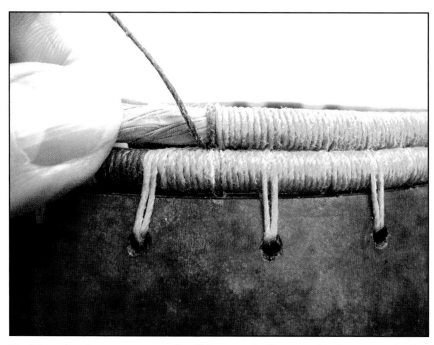

Find the color that you want, and pull it out to the front, under the core and other threads. Continue wrapping with the new color. It will catch the old color and lock it in after the first wrap.

Ending the Core

Whether you are doing one row to finish off a rim and accent a gourd, or twenty rows of complicated patterns, you eventually need to end the project. After all your work so far, this is not the time to become impatient.

As you begin your last row, you need to make your stitches closer together than you did on the previous rows. They were less compacted so that the anchor stitch would fit between them easily. On the last row, there is no need for this space. Cover the core tightly. This applies, also, if you are only doing one row.

Where you end the coil is based on where you started on the gourd. The rows of coiling will be uneven until you near the ramp area to the next row. Depending on whether you have level coils, or ones that loop up and down, the ending spot can be within a half inch of this location. By looking carefully you will be able to see the spot that the end will be least visible.

Decide if you need any of the extra colored threads for finishing the coil. You will be doing over-wrap anchors at the end for a few stitches and may need to change color if your design changes here. If you are done with the extra colors, cut the threads off before the end. Cut off the excess core, but leave an inch more than you need. You can always trim the extra, but you can't add a piece at the end. See the photos for details.

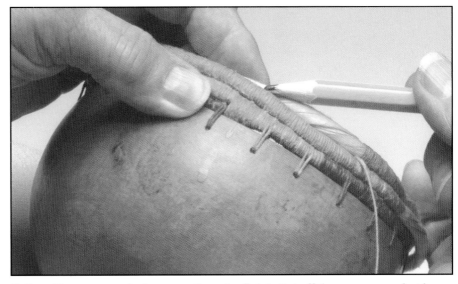

Coil until you are two inches away from the finish. Cut off the excess core, but leave an inch extra. Hold the core along the ramp, allowing it to slide behind the top row. Mark where the angle cut should go to make the coil level.

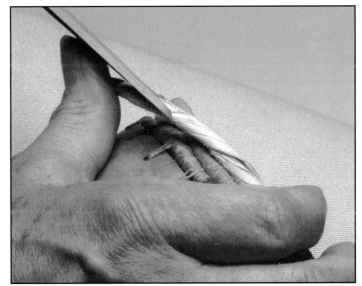

Cut along the outside of this line just a fraction, and see how it fits. Trim if necessary until the row forms a straight line. Cut off extra colored threads if you no longer need them to stitch into the pattern.

Coil as usual until you get to the start of the cut core. Use the needle to sew over-wrap anchor stitches from here to the end, keeping them very close together and pull them tight.

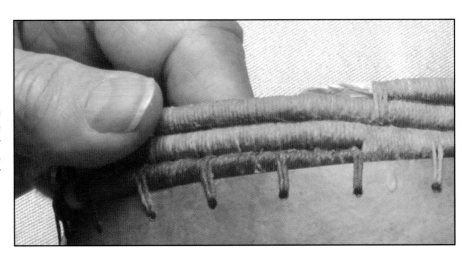

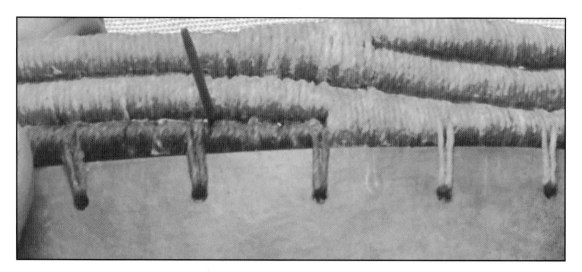

Keep wrapping for three or four stitches after the core is covered and do a figure eight anchor stitch to end. Cut off the thread. (You need to do several figure 8 stitches if you are using embroidery thread and add a touch of nail polish to the end.)

Handy Measurements

It helps to know how much material you are going to need to finish a project, so here are some measurements to keep in mind.

The amount of core needed to cover the edge using the size of the spoke pattern is approximately fifteen inches. Decide how many rows you need, multiply the distance of your rim opening by the number of rows of coiling, and add two rows for good measure. Always give yourself lots of extra core. You may decide on another row, or your coiling may flare outward, using more core than the base row.

The amount of waxed linen you need depends on the thickness of your core, and how closely you wrap each stitch. I'm giving you the lengths that I use with my tensioning. You may find this isn't right for you, so add extra. Find the core size below and multiply the length of thread per inch times the length of the core. To find out how much of each color you need, when working a pattern, figure out the number of spaces of each color on each row. Divide this into twenty-four to get the fraction. Twelve spaces of color out of twenty-four are half the distance. Work out the total amount of thread needed and divide that in half (or whatever fraction you got) for the amount of color. You don't need to do this for your projects; it just helps if you are running low on thread, or if you are getting a specific color from someone else.

Core Thickness	Thread per inch	Amt of Waxed Linen (4 ply)	Rows per inch
2/32"	12.5"	12.5 times length of core	8 rows
3/32"	13.5"	13.5 times length of core	7 rows
4/32"	15.5"	15.5 times length of core	6.5 rows
5/32"	18.25"	18.25 times length of core	6 rows
6/32"	23"	23 times length of core	4.5 rows

Of course if you cut the opening to a size other than the spoke pattern provided, you will need to do your own measurements. Just multiply the distance of your rim opening by the number of rows of coiling you want, and add at least two rows for good measure.

Chapter Four:

Projects

By following the instructions in *Chapter Three*, you can complete several rows of one or more colors. In *Chapter Four*, I deal with using all of these steps to create a project. I have tried to present projects that have skills that you can use in other work. Prepare the gourd as illustrated in the photos, or experiment with different finishes and colors. The same instructions used with different colors of thread, or different thicknesses of core, can result in surprisingly varied looks.

Project One:
Single row, three colors, six repetitions

Prepare your finished gourd as directed in *Chapter Two, 'Getting Started,'* by drilling twenty-four holes (see spoke pattern). Choose your three colors and decide which color will be your base color. I am using royal blue as my base, salmon as my second, and turquoise as my accent color. Choose a paper core (also known as fiber rush) that fits the thickness of your gourd. Because you are only doing one row, you need to cover the cut edge completely.

Finished gourd with one row, and six patterns

Cut three yards of each color of waxed linen, and thread the royal blue and salmon on tapestry needles so that the tails are about four inches long. Cut a length of paper core two feet long. Cut the end in an upwardly angled slant that spans one hole. Using your base color (royal blue), stitch from the inside of the gourd, about an eighth of an inch behind the slanted cut on the core, and through the first hole once. Tie a single knot tightly over the paper core and pull the knot to the inside of the gourd. Place the tail end of the knot along the core and hold it in place with your left index finger.

Take the other two colored threads and lay the unthreaded ends over the first stitch. Leave ¼" overlapping. From the inside of the gourd, stitch through the same hole for a second time, catching the two added colored threads, and pulling snugly. Hold the core in place and wrap the linen around the core using your right hand, by going over the top of the gourd and under your left thumb. Snug the stitch closely against the previous stitch. After 6 or 8 stitches, gently pull the added colored threads until the tails disappear. Do this slowly or they will pull out and you'll need to start over.

Continue wrapping until you reach the next hole. Make sure that no core is visible between the threads, and each stitch is straight and uncrossed. Use your needle to straighten the stitches up if necessary. Check that the two added colors stay flat along the core and don't peek out between the stitches.

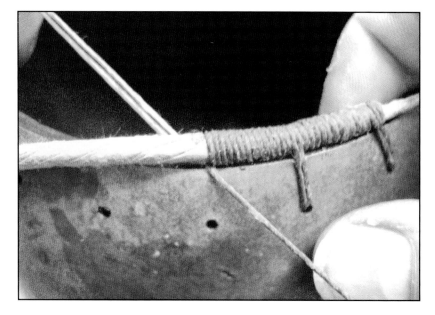

Stitch through the second hole twice with the base color and continue wrapping until you near the third hole, but do not stitch through it.

If your stitch count between holes is eighteen (including the anchor stitches at each end), you will now do 6 salmon, 6 turquoise, and 6 salmon between the third and fourth holes, starting by stitching with the salmon thread through the third hole twice. Adjust the number of wraps of each color so that the salmon is the same at the start and end of each hole (i.e.: 5 salmon, 4 turquoise, 5 salmon if the stitch count is 14; 5 salmon, 6 turquoise, 5 salmon if the stitch count is 16). Keep the stitches close together. Remember that to switch color, the working thread must cross over to lie along the back of the core, and the new thread must come from under the core, and both other colors (see notes on changing color).

After stitching with the salmon through the fourth hole, bring out the base color (royal blue) and wrap to the next hole and stitch twice through it. You have now coiled 4 sections, using 5 holes, and finished one repetition of the pattern. The pattern will be a blue section; a blue section; a two-colored pattern section, and a blue section. When you start the pattern again, you will then have three royal blue colored sections and a pattern. Repeat this pattern until you finish the rim. If done correctly, you will have six patterns with salmon stitched through the holes at beginning and end of the colored section, and ending with royal blue where it joins the beginning. The number of stitches between each hole may vary around the rim, so adjust your stitch count as necessary.

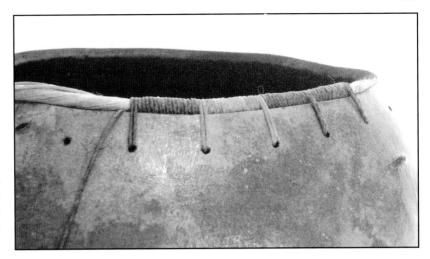

Add more of your base color thread as needed. When you are one hole before the beginning, lay the core along the edge behind the starting coil and mark with a pen where the two overlap. Trim and adjust the core to fit into the beginning slant. Wrap both ends of the core together, and trim off extra colored threads as soon as they are buried under the royal blue thread. Stitch a few stitches with the blue, into the beginning coil to bury the thread. Cut the thread close to the row, and push it out of sight (see 'Ending the core,' Chapter Three).

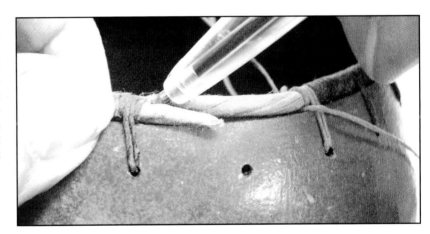

Use a hair dryer to heat the wax on the linen and turn it upside down on a flat surface. Rotate under pressure to level out the coil. The heat will melt the scuffmarks on the darker threads and make them uniform in color and shine. Pressing on the heated coils pushes the coils down to eliminate gaps.

Project Two:
Three Rows, three colors, four patterns

Prepare your finished gourd as directed in *Chapter Two, 'Getting Started,'* drilling twenty-four holes (see pattern). Choose your three colors and decide which color will be your base color. I am using emerald green as my base, sage green as my second, and country yellow as my accent color. Choose the thickness of the paper core that is best for this gourd and cut off enough for three rows, about five feet. You really only need four feet, but always give yourself a little extra.

I have base-coated this gourd in dark green and sponged on gold paint. It is sealed with a water-based finish.

Finished gourd with three rows, and four patterns.

Cut the core end in an upwardly angled slant that spans one hole. Thread all three colors on #18 tapestry needles so that the tails are approximately four inches long. Using your base color (emerald), stitch from the inside of the gourd, about an eighth of an inch behind the slanted cut on the core, and through the first hole once. Tie a double knot tightly over the paper core and pull the knot to the top of the core. This is different from the first project, because you will be burying the knot between the first and second rows of coiling. Place the tail end of the thread along the core and hold it in place.

Take the other two colored threads and lay the unthreaded ends over the first stitch. Leave ¼" overlapping. From the inside of the gourd, stitch through the same hole for a second time, catching the two added colored threads, and pulling snugly. Hold the core in place with your left thumb and wrap the linen around the core and the two colors using your right hand. Do this by going over the top of the gourd and under your left thumb. Wrap the stitches close to each other but not as closely as for the previous projects. You should be able to get a fingernail between threads. This is important because you need space to stitch from the row that will go above this. Make sure that the two added colors stay flat along the core and don't peek out between the stitches. The core should be barely covered and have no big spaces between threads.

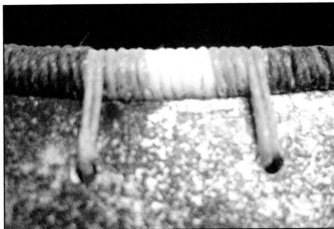

Continue wrapping until the second hole, and count the number of wraps you do between the holes. Either cut off the beginning ends of the added colors, or carefully pull on the threads until the loose ends disappear behind the wrapped stitches. Do this slowly or the threads will pull out and you will have to go back and do it again. Stitch through the second hole twice with the base color and continue wrapping until you reach the end of the second space (third hole), but do not stitch through it. The pattern begins here, so you will be stitching twice through the second hole with your second color (sage). Change thread color by moving the working thread (emerald) over the core, and bringing the sage thread out under the core and the other threads.

The third section is divided into three parts. Remember how many stitches you wrapped in the previous section and divide the stitches in this section as evenly as possible. Do not be too concerned about keeping the numbers exact, since you will be adding more stitches when you do the second row. The center part of this section will be yellow. This section should be evenly spaced threads of sage, yellow, and sage.

End the patterned section with the sage thread twice through the hole, and switch back to emerald. Wrap with the emerald through the next three holes. This will complete one pattern, filling 6 sections and using 7 holes. Continue with this pattern until you near the beginning of the coil.

Lay the core along the slanted beginning of the starting coil and stitch beneath the first coil, wrapping both cores together. Use your left thumb to hold the beginning core tight along the edge, and stitch between the gourd and the core. Start the stitch close to the first stitch that you put in at the beginning, and pull it back to ensure that you catch the end of the starting core.

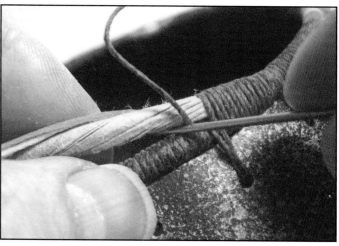

Stitch carefully until you cover the exposed core and have reached the beginning stitch and your thread is beside the beginning hole in the gourd. Stitch between the two anchor stitches from behind and between the gourd rim and the core on row one.

This is the start of the second row of coiling. Pull the thread to the front so that it comes out between the two cores. Take your needle and push the wrapped thread tightly between the two cores so that it touches the last wrap. The second row should be slanted in towards the center more than the first row. You do this by pressing your thumb against the core as you work. It helps if the gourd edge was cut on a slant as well.

Following your pattern, wrap half way to the next hole using the emerald thread. This will be 5 to 7 threads. Separate the threads on the row below and stitch below row one from the front through to the inside.

Bring the needle between the two cores going behind the anchor stitch that you just did. Pull tightly so that the thread slides between the stitches, front and back. This is a figure 8-anchor stitch, and you will be using it after every five to seven stitches, until the end of the project. Remember that an anchoring stitch is any stitch that holds the coil in place and can be an over-wrap stitch, a double or triple stitch or a figure 8 stitch.

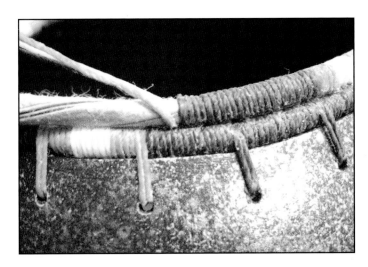

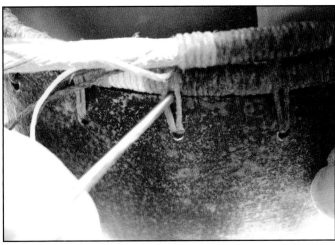

Following the pattern, wrap with the emerald thread to about the 3/4" mark of the next section. Switch the color to sage by moving the emerald thread over the core, and bringing the sage under the core.

Wrap with sage to above the next hole. This is directly over the first sage stitch. From the front, stitch between the gourd rim and the first row, going between the two anchoring threads. Bring the thread back between the two cores, and switch to yellow thread.

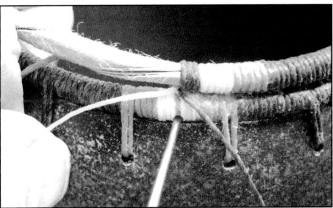

This section is divided into three; you will do a figure 8 in the middle and at each end. This is where you can make adjustments to the coiling in the row below. You can anchor as often as you wish if you need to cover the core below more thoroughly, or make the colored sections more even, but you must anchor at least once in the middle. The color changes should line up directly over the color changes on the row below. You may anchor at every color change, using the same color as below, or you may anchor in the centre using a two-color figure eight. I prefer to anchor every four stitches, because there are fewer gaps between the coils.

To do a two-color figure eight in this section, wrap the first third in yellow and switch to emerald thread. At the midpoint of this section, separate the stitches in the yellow coil below. Notice that you are using emerald thread, but need to anchor into yellow. If you use the emerald, it will be obvious, so you need to stitch with the yellow thread. This is a two-toned figure 8 stitch. Leave the emerald thread where it is, and pull the yellow thread out underneath the core and threads (as discussed in 'Changing Color' section). Use the yellow thread to do the figure 8 on the bottom and bring it back to the front behind itself. Pull tightly. Place the yellow thread along the core and continue coiling with the emerald thread. Pull firmly on the yellow to hold the core in place, because a two-color figure 8 is not as strong as the one color anchor. Do a figure 8 at the end of the section.

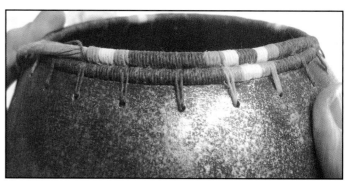

In the fourth section of the second row, begin with sage and wrap about one third of the section. Switch to emerald, and anchor in the middle and above each hole. Complete sections four and five in emerald thread, anchoring at midpoint and above each hole.

Section six is another two-color pattern, using sage and yellow. All your anchor stitches will be two-color figure 8's in this section. This will complete one repetition on row two. Continue around the coil until you reach the start of row three.

The third row is a repeat of the pattern on row one. This is also your finish row, so now you must make your wraps as close together as you can get them (see Project One). Anchor every 4 to 8 stitches, being careful to keep the number of stitches in the colored sections the same when you add the anchor stitch. Line up the start and end of each color section with the block of color below. I like to anchor at the start and end of each color change. The third row should be slanted in towards the center more than the second row. Notice that the stitches are uneven and scuffed at this point.

Finish the coil as described in project one, cutting off the extra colors in the last section. Use a hair dryer to heat the wax and press to level out the coil. To straighten out the stitches and even out the space between the coils, run the eye end of the needle firmly between each row, all the way around the coils. This combined with the heat and pressure will level the rows and flatten gaps. Notice that the scuffmarks have gone and the stitches are more even. If you wish, the gourd and coiling can all be polished with a coat of floor paste wax and buffed for a shine. You will need to heat again and run the needle between the rows to remove excess polish. Do not use liquid floor polish for this step.

Project Three:
Free-form with bead accents

Prepare your gourd by cutting an opening of any size, but big enough to insert your hand. Make the top with an irregular edge by dividing the opening into four sections. At every other section, dip the edge by at least an inch, to accommodate the selected beads. Avoid points since it is difficult to cover the core properly when it bends sharply. I have chosen a warty gourd with a sponge-painted finish, sealed with a water-based spray varnish. Choose a thread color that matches the finish on the gourd, and is complemented by the beads you have chosen. Select a core thick enough to cover the edge of the gourd; 5/32" diameter core works well on medium thick gourds. Gourds that are half an inch thick or more need to be sanded down on the inside to narrow the edge.

Painted warty gourd with coiling and bead embellishments.

Sand the cut edge to remove uneven spots, or the core will not lay flat on the edge. A sanding drum attachment on a dremel tool works well (center bit). When using a warty gourd, the bumps must be sanded off to allow for stitching. You can see the lighter areas where they were. I use a large structured-tooth cylinder with a 1/8" shaft (bottom bit).

Draw a line parallel to the edge and down 1/4" for the holes. Drill holes ½" to ¾" apart along the rim. I use the width of my baby finger for rough sizing. Holes may be closer together at sharp, inside curves, to hold the core more securely. Paint or finish as desired.

Cut the core end in an upwardly angled slant and attach to the gourd as in project two, with the knot on top. Start at the "back" of your piece, near the top edge of a dip. The overlap on the last row will be less obvious here.

Anchor twice through each hole with the over-wrap stitch as you coil completely around one row. This will take you longer than the previous projects because the distance is greater with the dips. On the second row, the coiling in the dips will not have anchor stitches, so the stitches need to be closely wrapped on these sections. Coil just to the center point of the first dip, anchoring after every 4 to 7 stitches with the figure 8 stitch. Stop to add your first bead embellishment.

Prepare the bead by using an eye pin as described in *Chapter 7, 'Embellishments.'* Stitch through the eyehole of the bead pin twice and anchor with a figure 8 stitch to the coil below. Allow the bead to fall inside the gourd as you continue to coil. You can also wrap the gourd in plastic wrap to hold the embellishment in place and keep the thread from catching. Remember that on the second row in the dips you do not need to leave space for anchoring, so wrap the stitches close together. (If you do not have eye pins, and the bead has a large enough hole to thread, then just coil two rows without the bead. Add the bead from the third row, and anchor down into the second row at the bottom of the dip. This is not the most secure because the edges of the beads can wear through the waxed linen after a while.)

Continue coiling and anchoring until the center of the next dip. Add another bead and continue around the gourd until you reach the top of the dip near the beginning of the third row. Do not coil down into the dip to start your third row, but anchor twice firmly at the top point. Free-coil the core (do not anchor) until it spans across to the top of the bead. Anchor through the eye pin through the bead twice.

Free-coil to the other side of the dip. Anchor twice firmly at the top of the next point, making sure that the coil is tight and the bead is straight up and down. If it isn't, unwrap back to the bead and reposition it. Continue around the gourd until you have spanned both dips and anchored the beads.

Make sure that the coil is centered on the gourd top and is symmetrical before anchoring at the last peak. Coil a second row around the circle for the fourth row and anchor twice at the second peak.

The fifth row will be a free-form row, so the stitches need to be tightly wrapped to completely cover the core. Decide how you want to form your free coil. You can wind it through the beads, or take it outside or inside the gourd. I chose to take it inside, and anchor it behind the bead. You could take it through the opening, across the bead, and back through the other side. Whether you anchor it or not is up to you. You may cut off any excess core here, if you know how much you need to finish.

This shows the top view of the anchor stitch at the top of the peak after the first dip. When you bring the coil back to the top of the gourd, it needs to anchor and then bend to go down for the second dip. Anchor with several figure eight stitches, whether you go inside or outside the gourd. Finish the other side in the same design as the first side, bringing the coil to the top of the last peak.

Once the coil is back on top, anchor firmly and bring to the top of the last row. This is the spot on the gourd where you originally began your coil; the top circle started; the first coil dropped down; and the last loop is now coming back up to complete one free-form circuit. It looks a bit like a busy freeway at this junction. That's why we started at the back of your gourd. Anchor again on the top coil and coil one more row. This will be the third row of coiling on the top, but is actually the sixth row of coiling on the gourd.

Cut off the core on a downward facing slant to fit into the contours of the top row just above the "freeway" in the last photo and end the coiling here. Heat and run the eye of the needle between the rows. Compress the rows by squeezing them between your fingers and also by using a flat item such as a ruler or spoon handle inside the dips to flatten the spaces between the coils. Manipulate the coils until they are a pleasing shape and position.

Project Four:
Danish cord or sea grass trim

Prepare your gourd by cutting an opening as shown, but big enough to insert your hand. Make the top with an irregular edge, with high points and low points, but no sharp bends. I have done three dips, all the same size, evenly spaced. Draw your guideline along the rim, 3/16 of an inch below the edge, and mark the holes about a baby finger's width apart (see *Chapter Two, 'Cutting and Marking'*). Finish the gourd as you prefer, but the sample is done using a floral decorative spray paint, and sealed with a matte spray sealer. The inside is done with hand-made paper in a matching color. Choose a length of Danish cord (or sea grass) that will go around the opening at least ten times. It is better to have too much and cut it off, than to run out. The Danish cord in this project was sprayed in sections with the floral decorative spray to match the gourd. Choose a thread color that matches or contrasts the finish on the gourd. The stitch you use is a basic interlocking stitch that spirals up the coil and looks like a chain.

Painted gourd with Danish cord trim.

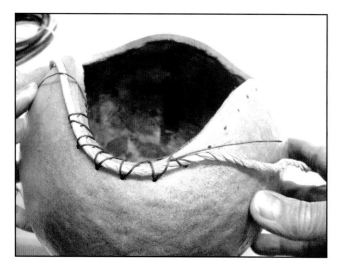

Start the Danish cord at the lower edge of one of the dips and leave a 6" to 8" tail. Lay the cord on the gourd surface, rather than on the cut edge as in previous projects. This gives the cord support that it needs because you will not be anchoring as often. Stitch through the hole once, and knot tightly, keeping the knot on the top of the core. Instead of wrapping the core with the waxed linen, as you did previously, stitch through the next hole twice, stitching from the front to the inside, and pull tightly. You will have one upright stitch, and one slanted stitch. Continue around the gourd until you get back to the start. Include the starting tail of thread in the wrapping to bury it.

As you begin the second row, stitch through the first hole again and then under the thread in front of the knot and under the core. From now on, you will stitch under each thread that you did on row one, without piercing the core. Pull tightly to hold the core in place, and push each stitch into line with the one on the row below. Continue around until you have completed three rows. Make sure that all the stitches are firm, and the core is slanting in towards the center.

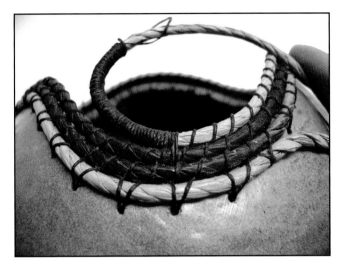

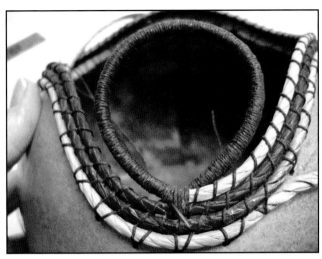

On row four, stitch the core until you reach the bottom of the first dip. Anchor the core with two over-wrap stitches and begin free coiling tightly around the core for several inches, until you can make a circle that partially fills the dip. My piece has loops that are 14.5 centimeters long. This is a good place to add more thread if you are running short. Otherwise, you need to knot the new thread onto the old thread at the back of one of the stitches.

Curve the coiled section around and behind itself and anchor firmly by doing at least four over-wrap anchor stitches where the core crosses, following the previous two anchor stitches in this spot. Bring the needle out between the two cores to begin wrapping from the front, and continue with row four. Stitch around the gourd top, doing a coiled loop at each dip, and stop coiling at the top of the last peak, near the beginning of row five. I have created three coiled loops.

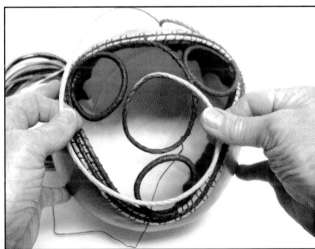

Anchor the core twice with over-wrap anchor stitches. Now you will span the space between the anchor point and the top of the coiled loop. Wrap the waxed linen loosely around the core, about the same spacing as you have been doing, until you reach the top of the first closed coil loop. Anchor twice with over-wrap anchor stitches. You may need to knot it at the back to keep the stitches in place.

At this point you need to make some decisions about the shape of your top. Depending on the size of your opening, you may be able to anchor back down onto the gourd again. Mine was too narrow at the top, so I chose to form an interlocking circular shape connecting the coiled loops.

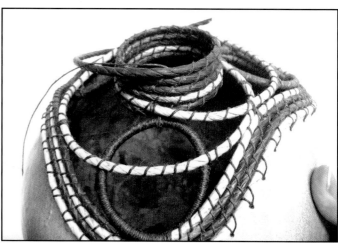

Wrap the core as you span the space to the other coiled loop and anchor again. Do the same to the third coil and anchor it. Decide how to interweave the core through the loops to make a pleasing pattern, anchoring each time the core passes over another core. It can get a bit awkward at this stage, so use pliers if you need them to reach inside.

When you have completed your design, cut off the bulk of the core and leave enough to create a finish. I have created a center tower of five rows of core, and now must bring the core to the front to meet the tail left at the beginning.

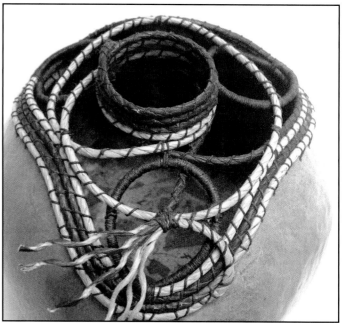

Stitch the core to any thread that it crosses as you bring it toward the front. Weave it through your loops for security as well as decorative effect.

Bring the first tail around and over the loop to meet the end tail. Stitch the tails together firmly, anchoring them to the coils below. Unwrap the ends of the Danish cord and spread them out. You may add more spray color if desired.

Chapter Five:

Advanced set patterns

Designing Geometric Patterns

As mentioned earlier, geometric patterns are based on repetitive patterns set up to span a set number of holes. For this reason, the 24-section spoke pattern provided in this chapter works well for most patterns. The twenty-four holes will give you a choice of six sets of patterns such as: two patterns of twelve holes; three patterns of eight holes; four patterns of six holes; six patterns of four holes; eight patterns of three holes; or twelve patterns of two holes. How you set up the design within these sets is up to you. I find that the minimum number of rows of coiling to make a pleasing pattern is three, and the minimum number of colors that work for me is also three. You, of course, are free to use as many rows as you want, and as many colors as you prefer. I'll give you the guidelines, and you create the finished product.

If you want numbers of patterns not found using the spoke such as five, seven, or ten repetitions, or a pattern that spans five or seven spaces, then you are going to have to calculate the number of holes you need. Do this by measuring around the top of your cut gourd, and divide it by the number of patterns you want. If you want five patterns, calculate that distance and mark it on your gourd in pencil. Divide these five segments into the number of holes your pattern needs and mark them. If the spaces between the holes are bigger than three-quarters of an inch, you'll need to make more holes. The spaces need to be between half-an-inch and three-quarters of an inch wide for best results. You will have to adjust your measurements accordingly. Draw your pattern on graph paper until you are satisfied.

I plan my patterns on my computer using a spreadsheet program. Using Excel, I adjust the column width to .5 (decimal point five) and that gives me little blocks appropriately sized for about six stitches. I count out twenty-four columns and mark off a dark line to represent with my hole marker (use the border selector in the format option). After I have marked my horizontal rows using the border settings, and marked my holes, I use the color selector to block out my designs. Doing this, I can create any number of rows or patterns desired. When I'm happy with my design, I copy and paste it together so that I can see what the finished project will be. This is how the patterns in this book were created.

If you don't have a computer, or do not use spreadsheet software, then graph paper works as well. The spaces are too big, so you need to divide them up into three or four sections. Do this on one sheet and then photocopy it for future use.

Draw darker upright lines evenly spaced to represent where the holes would be. Make your design to fit within the spaces between the holes. I like four repetitions of a pattern that spans six spaces and five rows high. I leave my first row plain, in the base color of my pattern and sometimes repeat that on the last row for balance, so my design would be three rows of colored pattern, with a solid colored row on top and bottom.

Graph paper works well if your design is only a few rows high, or doesn't curve in too much, but it doesn't work in all situations. If you want your coiling to taper sharply from the wide cut rim to a smaller opening, then each row will be smaller than the row before it. That means the patterns will start to get closer together, until eventually they touch and merge into one blob of color. If this is what you planned, that's great, but most times this isn't the desired result. To see what your design is going to look like if the coils slant in sharply (or flare out), you need to use a spiral graph. This comes courtesy of Darienne McAuley, who had this spiral drawn for her by a local architect. They are printed with approval from both parties. You may use them for personal use, but please do not use them for profit, without approval.

Make a copy of the spiral graph and put it inside a plastic page protector. Use washable markers to create your design on the plastic and adjust as necessary. Remember that you need to leave a hole in the center large enough to fit your hand into, and that your coiling is not going to be flat like the graph.

You are going to be working backwards on this one, because you need to draw in the last row first. Put your fist down in the middle of the graph and mark on either side for the opening. Draw around that spiral on these marks to form the last row of your work. Now count out the number of rows you want and mark the edge of your first row, where your design will start once you transfer to the gourd. Divide the graph into the sections you want and sketch your drawing between the edges you marked and the hole in the center. It is surprising how the design changes when it narrows toward the center. Keep adjusting until you get a pattern you like. Because your work will be at a different angle from the flat graph, you can't measure this design. Just use it as a visual reference and space your work accordingly. Start from the outside and follow the pattern in to the middle. If you make your coiling taper very sharply, it will look more like your graph, and will take the same number of rows to do. If you taper your coil more slowly, you can add more rows before you run out of space to work inside.

To make a pattern that flares outward, you go the opposite way. From the outside of the spiral, count in the number of rows you plan to coil and mark it for the starting row. Divide your graph into the number of sections you want and fill it in. Now your pattern will start in the center and go outwards. It will spread apart as it moves out, so you may want to add small designs in the last few rows. Again, your drawing is flat, but your coiling will probably be slanted. You decide how sharply the coils flare out, and this will change the size of the spaces between designs at the outside.

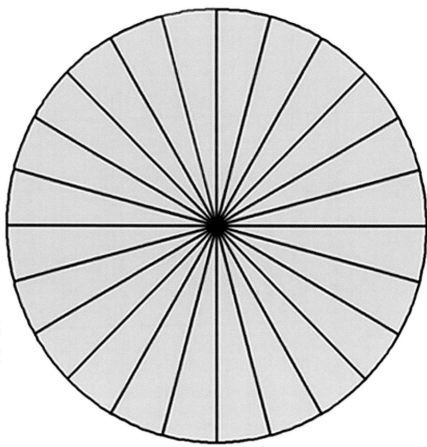

Circle measures 4.5" in diameter. Spoke pattern for marking 24 holes for coiling patterns based on 2, 3, 4, 6, 8 or 12 repetitions. Use only openings 4 to 5" in diameter.

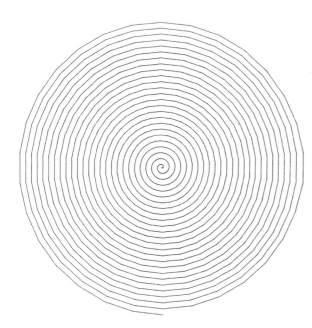

Darienne McAuley provided this spiral graph pattern. *Larry D Haight, Compudraft Design Services, Peterborough, Ontario, Canada.* **For full- size pattern see page 64**

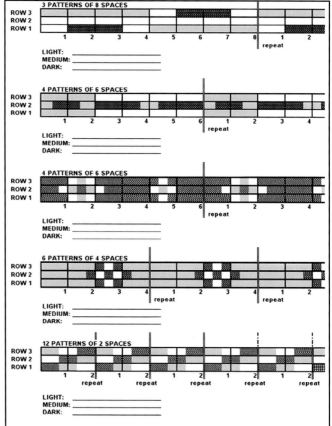

Selection of black and white patterns. By varying the color, you can significantly alter the look of the design. Write your color choices in so that you don't lose track. Place the sheet in a clear plastic protector and practice with different colors.

Selection of Greek motif patterns for a larger opening. Measure your rim; decide how many patterns you want; calculate the number of holes spaced ¾ of an inch apart, that you need to fit into that pattern size; mark the holes on the drawing to guide your stitches. Use a clear page protector to make it easier.

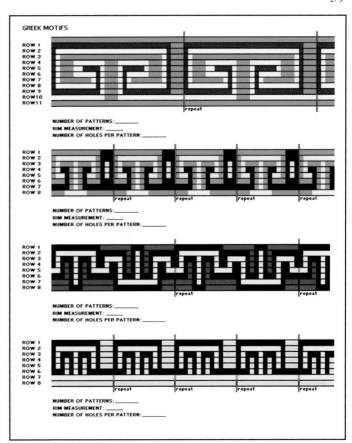

Selection of native patterns. Mark in the number of holes you need for your rim dimensions.

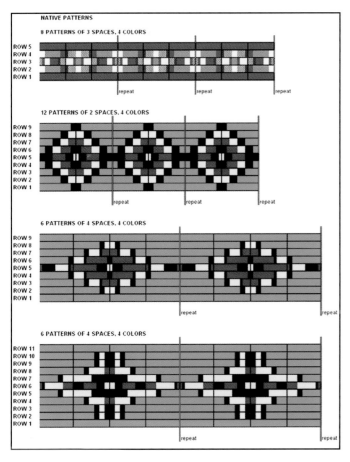

Selection of Celtic patterns. Mark in the number of holes you need for your rim dimensions. Use my markings, or make your own.

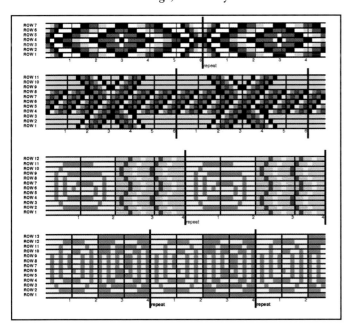

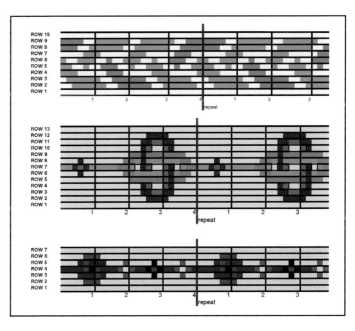

More geometric patterns. Mark in the number of holes you need for your rim dimensions. Use my markings, or make your own.

Designing Custom Patterns

Most of the time, I like to create a design that echoes or completes the work that I have done on the gourd. Remember that coiling is the last element, so plan before you start, so you know how many coils you want and what colors you need. Use the spiral graph if you plan to make the coiling taper or flare dramatically. Use the regular graph paper if you are going to coil fewer than six rows, or are going almost straight up.

I find it easier to select my waxed linen first and then find the paint to match. There are hundreds of shades of acrylic paint, or you can mix your own. Just be sure to mix up lots of paint so you don't run out. Colors never mix exactly the same way twice.

Sometimes, you may just want to let your color and coil shape wander. It's still a good idea to try to block out the colors to see if you like them side-by-side, or create a swirl pattern to follow. It's much easier to erase the marker from the plastic, than to unwind several rows of coiling.

You can make your own designs or borrow from clip art, but some shapes are not suitable for coiling. Square motifs, tribal basketry motifs, and some art deco are useful. Any stepped pattern such as cross-stitching or weaving can be adjusted but may lose definition. Diagonal, floral, or curved designs are not effective unless you are using #1 baby rush and twenty or more rows. Graphing your chosen design is a fast way to find out if it will work.

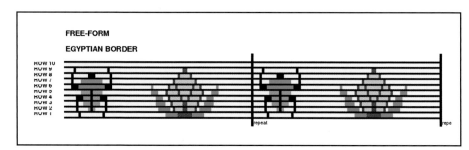

Free-form Egyptian border pattern. This pattern was an extension of the gourd pattern. See photos.

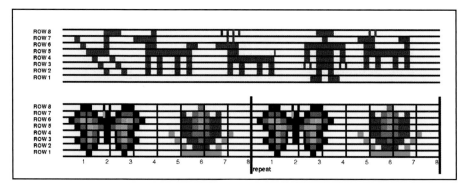

Free-form Native designs. These can be used singly or in a grouping.

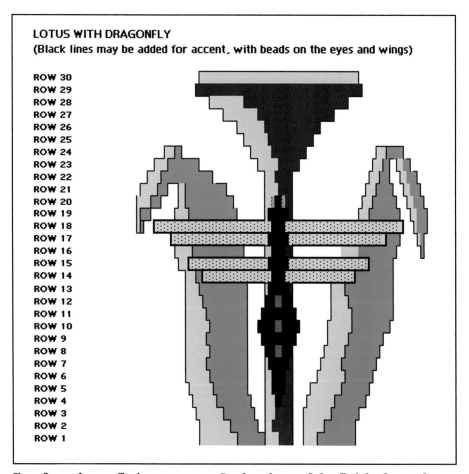

Free-form dragonfly inset pattern. In the photo of the finished gourd, you will notice that the stem on the lotus pod is much longer than in this pattern. See photos.

This is the dragonfly inset side of the completed gourd. This pattern was done up to the base of the lotus bud, as a separate tapestry piece and inset into channels carved inside the gourd walls. There are 36 rows, two of which are buried inside the bottom channel. The remaining 20 rows for the lotus pod tied the pieces together. The dragonfly was outlined in seed beads for accent, and echoed the beading on the rim. Note where the top is joined to the insert, there was a slight variation in the color of the waxed linen.

This is the design on both sides of the dragonfly gourd. The lotus design was burned into the gourd and then painted with acrylic paints. The motif coiled in the top is a stylized lotus bud.

This is the back of the dragonfly gourd. The dragonfly design was burned into the gourd and then painted with acrylic paints. The motif coiled in the top is a stylized lotus pod, and this side reflects the coiled inset in design.

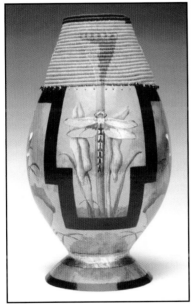

This is the Egyptian border motif shown on the finished gourd. The lotus buds are an extension of the design. The ten rows were the minimum I could use to create this design.

In this Egyptian design, the 8-row coiled base is also the base of the fans that divide the design on the gourd into sections. The 14 rows of coiling on the top are a series of colored rows that mimic the painted stripes on the top of the gourd. The top flattens out and has a repeat of the pattern shown on the base.

On this three sided art deco vase, the base is solid black, and the top has a Greek key motif, that narrows to a chimney, before flaring out to a flat top. The difficult part of this coiling was to take a triangular-shaped top and form it into a circle for the chimney. There are a total of 23 rows on the top, and 6 on the base. This was the second top that was done on this gourd. The first was removed because it didn't slant quickly enough into the chimney shape.

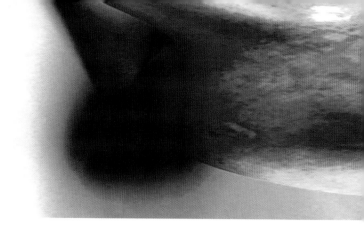

Chapter Six:

Other Coiling Techniques

Danish Cord

Danish cord is another type of fiber rush, but is created by twisting three strands of paper into one, giving it a rope-like texture. It is much more expensive than regular fiber rush, and is often colored either with spray or dyes. It is used in open coiling where the core material shows and the thread is used as an accent, rather than as the dominant pattern. It comes in the 4/32" thickness and is available at basketry or chair caning suppliers. For working a rim in Danish cord, see *Chapter Four, 'Project Four.'*

I was introduced to the use of Danish cord by Marla Helton of Indiana. She told me how to use decorative floral spray paint to color the Danish cord before coiling it. This product is available at craft stores and is specific for floral arrangements. I also experimented with water-based dyes and used that to color the Danish cord. I was concerned that the water would ruin the Danish cord, since it is made of paper, but the twist is so tight, that the color only penetrated the outside surface. I left some of it in the dye for up to an hour, and the only noticeable change was a slight thickening of the cord. If you were going to weave chair seats with it, I would avoid wetting the cord, but just for decorative use, I think dying or staining it will be fine. An added feature is that when you untwist the core, you get a tie-dye effect on the ends.

Both Marla and her partner Stuart Fabe create amazingly beautiful work using Danish cord. Some of their pieces are included in the photo gallery at the end of this chapter. The stitch that Stuart and Marla use is a long wrap stitch with a lock, worked from the front of the gourd to the inside. A description of this stitch can be found in stitch 14 of Peg Arnoldussen's stitch glossary found later in this chapter. The difference between the stitch shown in the glossary and the stitch you will use with Danish cord is that when using Danish cord, you wrap the entire bottom row instead of piercing it, as you do in pine needle coiling. You still work your needle through two stitches for each over-wrap.

Fabric Coiling

Any material can be used as a core or wrapping material, but for fabric coiling, it's best to use cotton clothes line material for a large coil, or cotton edging cord for a smaller coil, wrapped with long strips of material. Cut the material into half-inch strips and fold the edges under. Use a larger-eyed tapestry needle to thread the fabric. Wrap the cord with the fabric, overlapping the edge slightly five to eight times. Anchor by stitching an over-wrap stitch below the core in the previous row, just as you did for waxed linen coiling. You will be using the over-wrap anchor only and it will be much more obvious because of the width of the fabric, so maintain a consistent number of wraps between anchors. Add material the same as normal coiling.

Wire Coiling

Adding wire as an accent in coiling gives an element of surprise to the piece, but doesn't lend itself to large sections, due to the tendency of the wire to kink and unwind when released. Use a fine gauge wire in any color that complements your design and coil for a short section only, as an accent. Look for a soft wire that bends easily and holds its new shape. Decorative wire is often sold in packages of different colors and gauges (thickness). The rule is the higher the gauge, the thinner the wire. Wire that is 20 gauge or higher is thin enough to run through a large bead, and wraps easily but may break during wrapping. Wire that is 16 gauge or less, is too thick to bend easily, and won't hold its shape well. Experiment with different colors and thickness to add a new dimension to your work. Add new and end the wire sections just as if it were a new thread being added. Try to keep the ends at the back of the coil so that the bulk isn't as obvious.

Pine Needle Coiling

Dozens of books, booklets, pamphlets, and patterns have been written on pine needle coiling. I include the technique because it is impossible to talk about decorative coiling without mentioning pine needle work. The technique lends itself well to working on gourds, as the gourd provides the stable base and shape for the vessel, and the pine needles allow for a great range of creativity.

I have done coiling with pine needles, but I am definitely not an expert on this technique. The information included here, and the stitch glossary, was kindly provided by Margaret (Peg) Arnoldussen. For more information, techniques, patterns, and help, you can do an Internet search on her name, or go to her website at *http://pinebaskets.tripod.com*. She has included many links to other basketry networks. Another excellent source for basketry information is provided by Susi Nuss, who has thousands of links to help everyone from the beginner to the professional. Again, do an Internet search on her name or access her site at *http://www.basketmakers.org/*.

The materials used in pine needle basketry differ from closed coiling, due to the nature of the coils. Instead of a blunt tapestry needle, use large darning needles to pierce the raffia and pine coil. If you choose to do a stitch that needs to pierce the wrapping material, you need to choose raffia or sinew, rather than waxed linen, which will fray and break. All these materials are available at basketry or caning suppliers.

The stitches you do in pine needle differ from the closed coiling in that they actually pierce the core material itself. These stitches can be placed beside the stitch in the previous row, forming a running diagonal stitch, or completely separate from the stitches below making a broken pattern across the needles. In the case of the pierced stitches, the succeeding rows are stitched through the previous stitch, as well as the core, forming a linked chain stitch.

The type of pine needles used for your projects depends on the availability of needles in your area. The most desirable needles should be twelve to eighteen inches in length, with two or three leaves to a bundle. These are available from Torrey pines, Ponderosa pines,

Coulter pines, and Southern Longleaf pines found on the West Coast; and in the southern Atlantic states and the southeastern Gulf Coast. The sheath ends of the leaf bundles can be removed to form the core, or left on to be incorporated into the design. Late fall, just before the snow falls, is the best time to gather dried pine needles. Try to get the current year's crop of dried needles, rather than ones that have been on the ground too long. Wash them with mild detergent, spread them out to dry, and then store them in bundles wrapped with elastic or string where they can lay flat. If they do not bend into a loop when you want to use them, soak them in warm water for about an hour.

Depending on the type of stitch and the color of the binding material, you can form many variations of stitches to decorate your coiling. Try at least one pine-needle coiling project to add to your repertoire. Here is an excerpt from *Peg Arnoldussen's Stitch Glossary* and detailed description of each pictured stitch.

I stitch from front to back. I think it's much easier. Most of these illustrations, unless otherwise noted, depict the stitches in that way. About the only difference is that the stitch "arms" slant in the opposite direction. If you are a left handed coiler working from back to front, your "arms" will slant the same as these. Back to front stitchers probably pay a bit more attention to the "wrong" side of their work, thus making it more reversible. However, a front to back person can either learn to pay attention to their side-to-side stitch slant, or watch where the point comes out on the wrong side in order to be more disciplined about this (what I've done).

Stitches can easily be made reversible by paying attention to both the entrance and exit of the needle through the coil. When stitching from front to back, some stitches can be made reversible by inserting the needle at an angle to the right. Then watch the wrong side of your work to observe where it exits. Adjust slant to improve appearance. Some stitches look best on both sides if pierced straight through to back. Use your judgment in this.

Reproduced with permission from Peg Arnoldussen

Stitch 1: This is probably the most basic stitch out there. Execution is simply to loop over the coil, working toward the left, and then inserting into coil below. It will slant right and spiral if worked as I do it; it will slant left if worked back to front. Keep these stitches within ½ inch of each other or your basket will wobble. Each new stitch is worked just ahead of its corresponding stitch in the row below. *Courtesy of Peg Arnoldussen.*

Stitch 2: This is a pierced stitch. It is just like the one above except that it is worked into its corresponding stitch in row below, piercing it. (It works best using raffia or sinew, rather than waxed linen.) *Courtesy of Peg Arnoldussen.*

Stitch 3: This is much like Stitch 1 except that it is worked twice into same hole, producing a V with a right slanted and a vertical arm. This should be spaced a bit farther than the first stitch. *Courtesy of Peg Arnoldussen, graphics by Lea Galcso.*

Stitch 4: This is much like Stitch 3 except that the new stitch is placed ahead of the second arm of each V instead of between the arms. It is also the "wrong" side of Stitch 3, therefore very reversible. *Courtesy of Peg Arnoldussen, graphics by Lea Galcso.*

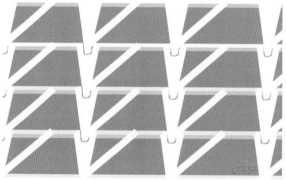

Stitch 5: This is like Stitch 3, but is accomplished by working from back to front. When worked this way, the V's will align vertically instead of spiraling, especially if you pull on the first arm of each new stitch, which will pull the right arm of the stitch below over to the right a bit more. *Courtesy of Peg Arnoldussen.*

Stitch 6: This stitch is also much like Stitch 3, except that the vertical arm of each V is pierced. In back-to-front stitching, the vertical arm will be the first or right arm. The stitches will align vertically. *Courtesy of Peg Arnoldussen.*

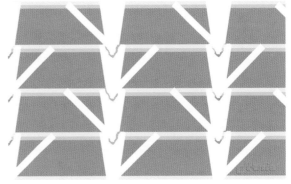

Stitch 7: In this case, the slanted arm of each V is pierced, which will cause the stitches to spiral sharply. Back-to-front will spiral to left. *Courtesy of Peg Arnoldussen.*

Stitch 8: This is much like Stitch 6 except that the rows are worked alternately; Row 1: front to back, Row 2: back to front. *Courtesy of Peg Arnoldussen.*

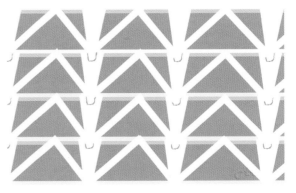

Stitch 9: This is very much like Stitch 2 except that it is backstitched. Backstitching must be worked at the end of every round to be backstitched. When the round is completed, go back around in the opposite direction, inserting into every hole already made, to the end of that round, which is where you then start the next row of new coiling. Backstitching adds an arm that slants in the opposite direction of the slant achieved on the initial round. *Courtesy of Peg Arnoldussen.*

Stitch 10: This is very much like Stitch 6 except that it is backstitched. See instructions for Stitch 9. Backstitching, in this case, adds a mirror image arm to opposite side of stitch. *Courtesy of Peg Arnoldussen.*

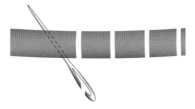

This diagram is looking down onto the top of the coil with the back of the coil being at the top of the diagram, and the front being at the bottom. It shows how the needle is angled as it pierces the coil below, catching the stitch in the previous row (see next diagram). *Courtesy of Peg Arnoldussen, graphics by Lea Galcso.*

This is a vertical chain stitch used in work by Stuart Fabe and Marla Helton. This stitch, contributed by Pamela Zimmerman of North Carolina, is very useful because it provides vertical alignment in a straight stitch. Its execution, however, is quite different from everything previously described, so illustrations follow. This presentation is front-to-back, but it can easily be worked from back-to-front. Remember that the insertion point must be before the corresponding stitch below, the needle is angled forward and exited after the next stitch below. Thus, the resulting loop wraps perpendicular to the coil. *Courtesy of Peg Arnoldussen, graphics by Lea Galcso.*

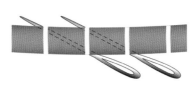

This diagram shows you the position of the needle as it pierces the row below. The needle on the right indicates the first stitch, as it passes under the front of one stitch, and out under the back of the second stitch. The needle on the left shows how the next stitch goes straight over the coil, and through the front of the stitch just used. In this technique, you will stitch through the row below under the same stitch twice, once on the back, and once on the front. *Courtesy of Peg Arnoldussen, graphics by Lea Galcso.*

Chapter Seven:
Tips and Tricks

By now you will have discovered what works well for you and have developed a style of your own. You will also have run into a number of frustrating problems that you may or may not have solved. Listed below are some things that I have discovered from working with dozens of people over the years that may be of help to you.

Also I have included a section on coiling for left-handed people. There are always obstacles being a 'lefty' in a right-handed world. Most of us adapt early and never really pay attention to the difference, until we run into a technique that just doesn't work as well for left-handers. One of those I tried and failed at miserably was calligraphy. You just can't do it easily, because you drag your hand through the ink and smear it all over the page. The teacher had obviously never had the problem come up, because he was amazed that I was having problems. His suggestion was to print backwards from right to left. My solution was to leave calligraphy to someone else. Unlike calligraphy, coiling does not present too many problems, and they can be solved with a little extra care.

Coiling for 'Lefties'

It is a right-handed world, and for the majority of people, that's fine, but for 12 to 15 percent of the population, this presents some problems. The percentage may even be higher among crafters and artisans, since the right brain controls the left hand, as well as being the base of creativity. It stands to reason that a lot of artistic people are left-handed. I have one or two left-handed people in each of my classes, and it is rare for me to have a class with all right-handers. I have had to learn to coil right-handed so that I can teach both groups, but occasionally I have erred and taught my class to coil left-handed. It's not a serious problem, though, since you just need to switch directions. All the instructions are the same sequence. We 'lefties' do this reversal all the time.

The most serious problem is the safety issues involved. Tools and machines are made to be used with the right hand. Using them with the left often exposes the user to hazards that can cause serious injury. I have nearly cut off my right arm with a power saw, because I was having trouble seeing the line on the wrong side of the blade, and didn't notice that my arm was in the path of the blade. Also, power-carving tools rotate in a clockwise direction and right-handed people pull towards them when carving. Left-handed people must push away from themselves, and it's hard to see what

you are doing. You can get reversible drills, but of course, the drill bits are cut for right-handed use, so this is only an advantage on a burr-type drill bit that has no directions of use. Many tools have the power switch on the thumb side for right-handed users, so it's awkward to shut off the tool if you are left-handed. Being a 'lefty' means exercising extreme caution when using power tools, because we are naturally more awkward using them.

Much safer, but still frustrating is the construction of some craft materials. Fiber rush or paper core is mechanically twisted, as is the 4-ply waxed linen. You guessed it, it's wound backwards for left-handed use. That means that all the time a 'lefty' is coiling, the core and waxed linen are unwinding. The result is that the paper core gets thicker and looser, and loses its definition, making the rows uneven. The only solution to this problem is constant vigilance. Keep the excess core wrapped in a coil secured with an elastic band and tuck it under your right arm or leg. Every few inches, twist the whole bundle of core back the opposite direction to tighten the twist. After a while it will become automatic and you won't even notice you are doing it. Of course, cutting the fiber rush on an angle to start or stop your coil will go in the opposite direction of the twist. Either use very sharp scissors to cut through the twisted layers, or trim the core a bit at a time.

The thread is another problem, because the wrapping motion around the core unwinds the thread at a rapid rate. The result is a thread that wraps around itself and ties into knots when you try to do an anchor stitch. My solution is to pinch the thread between my thumb and index finger as it exits the coil, and slide my hand along the length of the thread, allowing the needle end to spin freely, removing the kinks. On shorter lengths of thread I spin the needle between my fingers and watch the kinks fall out. Only work with six to eight feet of thread at a time. More than that and you'll spend longer untwisting and unknotting than you will spend in coiling.

The coiling position is opposite to the instructions given earlier, but if you are a 'lefty' you automatically switched anyway, so this is just confirmation. Sit with the gourd in your lap, the core along the edge and end pointing at your left hand. Tie the core on and wrap by bringing your left hand towards your chin, over the top of the gourd and under your right fingers and thumb. Pull the thread sideways to the left to snug the stitches. Use the index finger on your right hand to push the stitches into place and apply pressure with your right thumb to create the inward slant of the coiling.

When you work left-handed, the core has a tendency to unwind. This makes the rows uneven, and throws your patterns off.

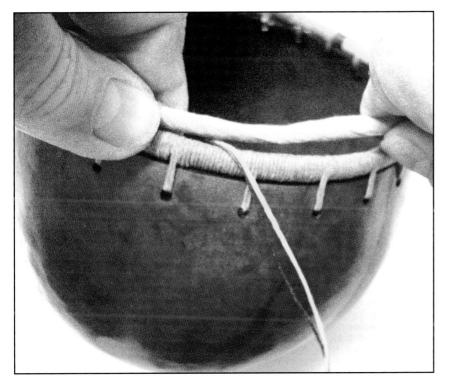

When the core loosens, hold the end away from the gourd, and twist until the core tightens again. Make sure that the extra core is wrapped and held with an elastic band, and rotate the bundle every so often, to maintain the twist.

To unwind thread that has twisted, run the length of the thread through your fingers, from the gourd out to the end, and allow the needle to spin freely to untangle.

Waxed linen

Dye lots vary considerably, so keep the roll of thread you are using inside your project when you aren't working on it, and wrap unused thread back onto the roll. If you have more than one roll of a color, they may not be exactly the same shade and you won't notice that you have used a different roll until you've done a big section. Order at least two of each color if you are planning several projects.

Also, waxed linen knots easily. Work with two or three arms-lengths (6 to 8 feet) of thread at a time. More than that and it gets tangled; less than that and you are adding thread constantly. Once you get a knot, do not pull it through the coil because the wax will form a solid lump and you will just have to cut the thread and start a new piece.

Threading the waxed linen through the eye of the needle is easier if you pull the end of the thread between your fingernails to flatten it (or your teeth, if you are like me and stick everything in your mouth). Some waxed linen is waxier than others. For some reason the black seems to have more wax than the other colors. Unless you are ambitious and feel like unwinding and ironing the thread between paper towels, there isn't a lot you can do about it until you are done. Heating the coiling with a hair drier melts the wax, and you can blot some of it off then. I keep baby wipes handy to wipe my hands frequently because I don't like the feel of the wax build-up on my hands. It also helps to keep the lighter colors from getting too soiled, although I have yet to discover how to keep them pristine and clean when doing larger sections. The lighter colors seem to absorb the dye from the other threads and get grungy-looking very quickly.

Organization

It is difficult, if not impossible to coil in a cluttered area. The neater you are, the easier it is. I wrap my extra core with a rubber band, and tuck it behind my back or under my leg while working. I also have a sequence of changing color. I always throw the old thread over to the opposite side before I pull out the new thread, so it's always an over/under sequence. This minimizes the tangling of the threads. If I'm working in an upholstered chair, I stick my needles into the arm when I'm not using them so that they are handy, but out of the way. If there is no upholstery, I stick the needles in my clothing, or as often as not, in my mouth. This is not a recommended habit to develop.

I often coil while riding in the car, so I devised a usable container with which to work. I use a plastic storage container about eight inches wide, five inches deep, and thirteen inches long to hold my needles; an awl; a measuring tape; small tapestry scissors; note-pad; pencil; patterns; extra core; and thread. It's easy to carry, and I can work right on the lid of the container when I'm riding in the car. All my needles are inside an old film container, or stuck through a small piece of material. I use a plastic container that came with salad greens in it, but a large margarine tub would work as well. A magnet comes in handy too, in case you drop the case. The magnet holds the scissors, awl and needles in one spot, or helps to pick up the needles when they drop between the seats of the car.

When the threads become tangled with the core, it's easier to pull the core through the tangle than to try to unwind each needle.

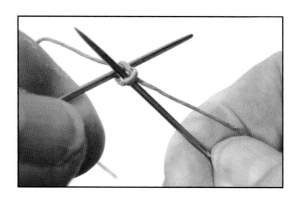

To undo a knot, catch it early and use two needles to separate the strands. Push the needles into the knot from opposite directions and gently pull the knot open.

My portable coiling supply box is an empty salad green container. It's clear so that I can quickly find my supplies and the top is large enough that I can work on it. It is self-contained and easy to carry.

I'll add a note here for 'lefties' when coiling in the car. Be careful with that needle when pulling through an anchor stitch. My poor husband fears for his safety as my flailing arm waves perilously close to his face. It makes for unsafe driving circumstances if he keeps flinching and ducking.

Lighting

To see the stitches properly, especially the dark colors, natural daylight is best. If you can't work in daylight, the next best thing is fluorescent ceiling lights that are often used in workshops and kitchens. My studio has three of them, but I prefer to work outside when possible, or near the window. For working at night when I'm traveling, I use a portable craft lamp with halogen bulb. These are sold at beading and crafting stores under the trade name of OTT-LITE®.

When I can't use natural daylight, or don't have access to fluorescent lighting, I use my OTT-LITE®. It is small, lightweight, and easy to pack.

Splicing core

No matter how well you plan your project, things can change mid-work and you find that you don't have enough core. You can splice, but it is really hard to hide a join. Try to position it where it won't be obvious, or add an embellishment to cover it.

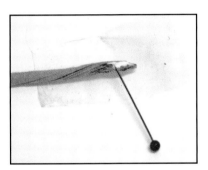

Cut the old core on an angle, and the new core on the opposite angle so that they complete each other. Lay the old core down on the sticky side of a short piece of scotch tape and with a Q-tip or pin tip add a tiny drop of white glue. Try not to let it run, you just want a small bit to moisten the paper.

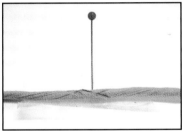

Lay the new core carefully on top, matching the cut angle and hold it down with a pin.

Wrap the tape up the sides and join the tape as close to the edge of the core as possible. Trim the tape when the glue has dried (usually takes an hour).

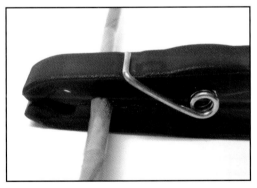

I sometimes clamp a clothespin over the join so that the core runs through the small hole in the center of the clothespin. This compresses the join. This clothespin has a selection of various size holes, allowing me to use it on different sizes of coil.

If you are using baby rush, put a small piece of scotch tape on the back of both cut ends. Cut the angles as long as possible to give you more joining surface.

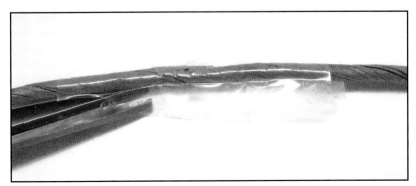

Add a tiny drop of glue, position carefully, and stick the two pieces of the tape together. Trim when dry.

Coiling a Base

Coils make a nice base, but you have to make sure that your gourd is level. You can draw around the base with a marking instrument like you use to level the top, or you can set the gourd on a container that is three or more inches across and draw around that, after you have used a level to set the line. I sometimes use brass rings that I have for macramé or Tenerife designs to mark my circle.

Stitching under the base coiling is awkward because of the curve of the gourd, and if you have a painted finish, all that digging around with the needle can mar it badly. You may need to do some touch-ups here, if you plan to paint that area. It's best if this area is left with the natural gourd finish.

Make the base between four to eight rows of coiling. Either make it plain, or add a pattern to match the rest of your gourd.

You can use anything round to help you outline your base attachment. Just make sure that it is level before you drill the holes, or your gourd will be tilted on its base. This is a macramé or Tenerife ring. You can use tubs or large-mouthed jars.

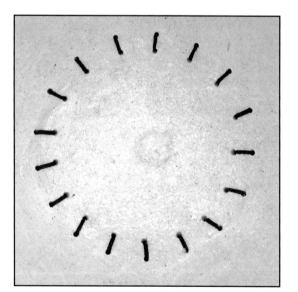

This is how the base attachment looks from inside the gourd. Drill holes on both sides of the circle that you marked, so that they are a quarter of an inch on either side of the circle or half an inch between the outer ring and the inner ring. The outside holes will be a little farther apart than the inside holes. One of my students suggested that these holes be drilled on an angle slanting in towards each other so that it is easier to get the needle through.

Use a curved tapestry needle to get under the coils on the base when working the second and third rows. Obviously you have to have an opening big enough to get your whole hand inside the gourd to work, so work the base before you coil the top. Either paint the inside to cover the stitches, or decoupage the inside.

Working with Embellishments

Gourds are a natural item and lend themselves to more natural embellishments such as feathers, leather, seeds, nuts, plant fibers, and stone-type beads. To attach these items to the working coiling, you need to drill holes through them so that the thread will pass through. These items need to be anchored firmly with several stitches to keep them secure. If you want to add them later, then you need to wire them for attachment. For glass or stone beads, the edges may be sharp and you risk cutting the thread if the bead moves or rubs against the surface. For these beads, I use eye pins to form an anchor at each end of the bead.

If you are adding the beads or embellishments while you are coiling, it is going to cause problems with the working thread. Each time you wrap the thread around the gourd you are going to catch the embellishment. You are either going to break the thread, break the embellishment, or both. To minimize the frustration, wrap the gourd in plastic wrap and cover each embellishment as you add it.

If you have seed cases such as Jacaranda pods or Deodar pine roses, drill small holes and thread fine-gauge wire through. Add beads to cover the wire.

Twist tightly in the back and wire directly on to the finished coiling.

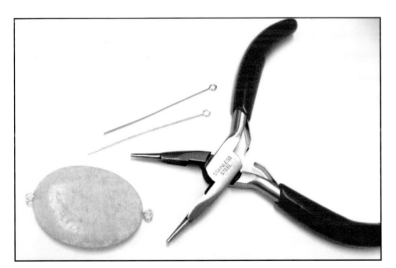

Not all beads have a hole large enough for a tapestry needle to pass through. Use eye pins available at beading or craft stores and insert the pin through the hole of the bead, or seed. Form another eye, or circle at the other end of the bead, using round nose pliers and cut off the excess shaft. Use a drop of instant glue inside the hole along the pin to keep the bead from spinning. Don't glue your fingers to the bead. When the glue has dried, stitch the bead to the coiling using the eyes on each end.

You'll want to wrap the warty gourd with clear plastic food wrap because the entire surface of the warty catches the thread as you coil. If you are adding embellishments, cover them with the wrap as well.

Slanting the Coil

The slant of the coil is dictated by the angle that you cut the gourd rim and the pressure you apply while coiling. While wrapping, apply pressure with your left thumb against the working core. Position your fingers properly, with the thumb against both the working coil and the row below, and the index and middle finger inside the gourd. Press down on the top of the coil with your index finger when you anchor, and pull tightly. That holds it firmly in place. Check often that the rows are slanting evenly.

In order to help your coils slant towards the center of the opening, cut the edge on an angle facing down into the gourd. If you want the coils to go straight up, then cut the edge flat.

The angle of the coils can be sharp, straight up and down, or out, depending on how you control the core with your thumb.

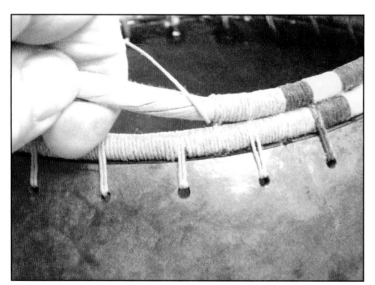

If you find that your walls still don't slant in, you are probably just holding on to the loose core while wrapping, rather than having your thumb against the gourd wall or coil, and your index and middle finger against the inside of the coil or gourd. This causes two problems. First, the coils don't slant in, and second, the anchor stitches won't be tight enough, so that there will be space between your rows.

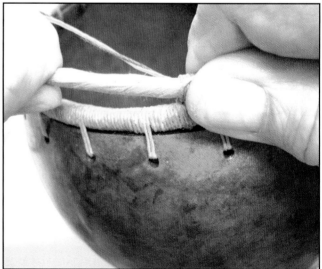

After every couple of anchor stitches, stop and check the slant of your coil. If it's still not slanting in, grip the stitches tightly in your right hand, twist the loose core to tighten it with your left hand, and pull hard. This will move the core a tiny bit inside the stitches, and make the top row a bit smaller than the one below. Do this often, or your anchor stitches will be pulled out of position, and your row will be lopsided.

Dressing/Finishing tips

To dress your work, or make your finished coiling present itself in the best possible light, there are a couple of tricks to use. You have already read about using the hair dryer to melt the wax and make the thread shiny. You have practiced turning your flat piece upside down and compressing it to level the top row and minimize the end join. You need to practice using the needle to straighten the stitches and bury the anchor threads and color changes. I spend a lot of time when I'm finished my coiling, dressing my work. Study your coiling from all angles and push and prod it until it suits you. Make the opening as round as possible, or as even as possible if your opening is not a circle. Once you are happy, set it aside and enjoy it.

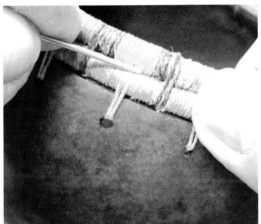

Use the eye end of the needle and press it firmly between the rows, following the coiling all the way from the bottom to the top, and back down going the opposite direction. This does three things. It removes excess wax if you polished your finished piece with floor paste wax; it straightens up gaps in the stitches caused by anchoring; and pushes loose anchor stitches back so that they are less visible. You can see all the excess wax flakes on the thread. This will melt when heated and become shiny.

Now you can use the tip of the needle to push extra tail ends between the rows, and move threads from changing colors into a better position.

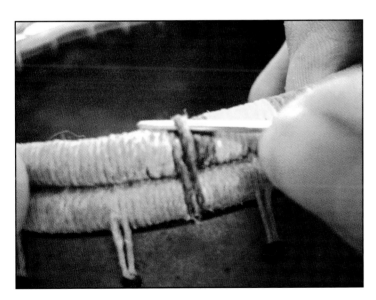

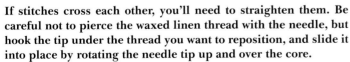

If stitches cross each other, you'll need to straighten them. Be careful not to pierce the waxed linen thread with the needle, but hook the tip under the thread you want to reposition, and slide it into place by rotating the needle tip up and over the core.

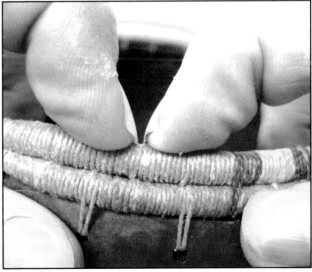

Unless you deliberately made your rows using the lacy stitch, you will want to eliminate spaces between rows, as it detracts from the overall design. If heating, compressing and running the eye of the needle around the coils didn't work, heat the coiling again and use your hands and fingers to press and manipulate the coils until you can close the gap. If it is an undulating coil design, you can use a curved item such as a shoehorn, dowel, spoon or anything with a curved edge to press the coils into place. Perfection isn't necessary; just try to eliminate really obvious spaces.

Gallery

Contributing Artists' Work

These next photos are examples of art done by other fiber artists. Most are done on gourds, but a few are not. These were included to show you examples of beautiful workmanship that can be incorporated onto gourds as well. I hope that this section gives you encouragement to try something new and to experiment with other media in your work.

'The Hive.' Plain gourd, using larger core. Separate lid has a raised portion of the coil forming a handle on top; 8" by 6.5". *Courtesy of JoAnne Abreu, from the collection of Leah Comerford.*

'Sunburst' using waxed linen on a chip-carved, stained gourd; 6" by 8". *Courtesy of Barbara Bellchambers.*

'Woman's Gourd' using waxed linen on a chip-carved, stained gourd; 12" by 8". *Courtesy of Barbara Bellchambers.*

'Petroglyph' using waxed linen on a stained pyro-engraved gourd; 12" by 8". *Courtesy of Barbara Bellchambers.*

'Untitled.' Gourd base decoupaged with rice paper, waxed linen on large core; 6" by 5". *Courtesy of JoAnne Abreu, from the collection of Leah Comerford.*

'Untitled.' Gourd base decoupaged with rice paper, waxed linen on large core. Beads and disk embellishment; 6" by 5.5". *Courtesy of JoAnne Abreu, from the collection of Leah Comerford.*

'Black Maria.' Natural Danish cord with painted gourd. *Courtesy of Stuart Fabe.*

'Great Spirit Turtle.' Gourd base is pyro-engraved and painted, with waxed linen on small core; 6" by 7". *Courtesy of Darienne McAuley, from the collection of Leah Comerford.*

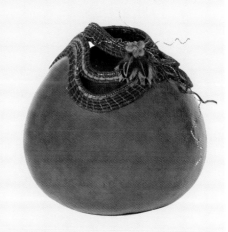

'Autumn Bounty.' Colored Danish cord with metallic thread and embellishments. *Courtesy of Marla Helton.*

'Sanctuary.' Natural Danish cord on plain gourd. Smaller gourd inside the cavity. *Courtesy of Stuart Fabe.*

'Coil Divine.' Colored Danish cord with colored wire and embellishments. *Courtesy of Marla Helton.*

'Rainbow Harmony.' Colored Danish cord with twisted silk and metallic embellishments. *Courtesy of Marla Helton.*

'Uprising.' Natural Danish cord on partial gourd. *Courtesy of Stuart Fabe.*

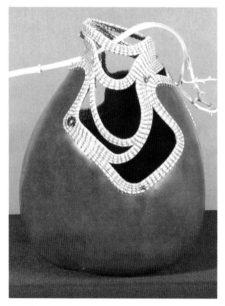

'Sculptural Harmony.' Natural Danish cord with twig and bead embellishments. *Courtesy of Marla Helton.*

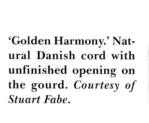

'Golden Harmony.' Natural Danish cord with unfinished opening on the gourd. *Courtesy of Stuart Fabe.*

'Autumn Shimmer.' Gourd with leather dye spots, coiled with pine needles, dyed raffia and shell embellishments. *Courtesy of Pamela Zimmerman.*

'Conversing with the Lorax.' Gourd with acrylic wash/shoe polish. Coiled with paper rush and mixed fibers, including acrylics, polyester, feathers, cotton, wool, acetate, waxed linen binder, glass beads and shell embellishments. *Courtesy of Pamela Zimmerman.*

'Drifted.' Gourd with watercolor wash/shoe polish. Coiled with Procion®-dyed hand processed yucca fiber, bound with waxed linen. Driftwood handle and shell embellishments. *Courtesy of Pamela Zimmerman.*

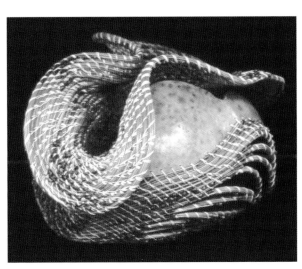

'Mandarin Maze.' Natural gourd coiled with philodendron sheaths and artificial sinew, and embellished with brass bits and coins. *Courtesy of Pamela Zimmerman.*

Close-up of the inside of 'Emanation,' showing the open bottom and inside as the coils come up through the center. *Courtesy of Pamela Zimmerman.*

'Emanation.' Gourd coiled with pine needles and artificial sinew. Coiled from the bottom of the cut gourd, downward, and then up through the center of the gourd. *Courtesy of Pamela Zimmerman.*

Close-up of the inside of 'Gabravanel,' showing the coiling detail in the bottom. *Courtesy of Pamela Zimmerman.*

'Gabravanel.' Gourd and pine needles dyed with Procion® dye and coiled with sinew. *Courtesy of Pamela Zimmerman.*

'Wound up Tight.' Natural gourd, with free-form coiling using pine needles and waxed linen. *Courtesy of Peggy Wiedemann, photography by Jan Seeger.*

'Coming Together.' Natural gourd pieces are joined together with free form coiling using pine needles and waxed linen. *Courtesy of Peggy Wiedemann, photography by Jan Seeger.*

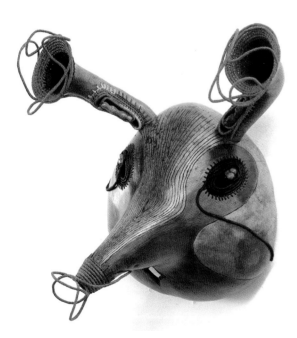

'The Forest has Ears.' Gourd mask using waxed linen over small core. *Courtesy of Wally Szyndler, photos by Stefan Bauschmid.*

'Yellow Warty.' Natural finish warty gourd, using waxed linen over small core. Embellished with tagua nuts. *Courtesy of Wally Szyndler, photos by Stefan Bauschmid.*

'Circle of Friends.' 2-ply silk thread lightly waxed, hand painted variegated silk thread, lightly waxed, glass and sterling silver beads, coiled over small paper core (paper rush); 6.25" across .5" deep. *Courtesy of Judy K. Wilson*.

'Fiesta.' 4-ply silk thread lightly waxed. Coiled over small paper core with glass and copper beads; 5.5" wide. *Courtesy of Judy K. Wilson*.

'Star Swirl.' 4-ply silk thread, lightly waxed, over paper core (paper Rush); 8 to 9/16" diameter. Took one month to complete. *Courtesy of Judy K. Wilson*.

'Rendition.' 1-ply silk thread, lightly waxed over tiny core (lead core line), sterling silver beads & glass beads; 3-1/8" across and 5/16" deep. *Courtesy of Judy K. Wilson*.

'Mimbres.' 4-ply silk thread, lightly waxed, copper rings, glass beads, paper core (paper rush). 3-1/8" high x 3-7/16" across at widest point. Opening is 2-15/16" across. *Courtesy of Judy K. Wilson.*

'Big Step, Little Step.' Paper core (paper rush), 4-ply silk thread, lightly waxed; 4.5" by 5/8" deep. *Courtesy of Judy K. Wilson.*

'Ancient Steps.' Gourd base is pyro-engraved, dyed, painted, and coiled with waxed linen on small core. The pattern is an extension of the base. *Courtesy of Darienne McAuley.*

'Spiraled Lights.' 4-ply silk thread, lightly waxed, glass, Aurora Borealis beads, small paper core (Paper Rush). The beads are somewhat faceted and seem to light up as you turn the basket. I found the beads and then made the basket around them. *Courtesy of Judy K. Wilson.*

'Man in the Maze.' Gourd base is dyed, painted, and coiled with waxed linen on small core. The coiled pattern is the focal point of the design. *Courtesy of Darienne McAuley.*

'Spirit Portal I.' Gourd base is dyed and pyro-engraved with cutouts and coiled with waxed linen on small core in a repeating motif. *Courtesy of Darienne McAuley.*

'Homage to the Southern Apache People.' Gourd base is pyro-engraved, dyed, and coiled with waxed linen on small core in a repeating motif. *Courtesy of Darienne McAuley.*

'Great Spirit Turtle II.' Gourd base is pyro-engraved, dyed, painted, and coiled with waxed linen on small core. *Courtesy of Darienne McAuley.*

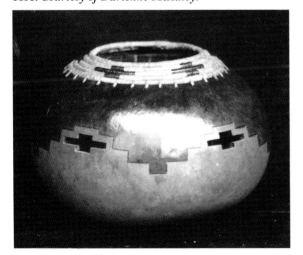

'Spirit Portal II.' Gourd base is dyed and pyro-engraved with cutouts and coiled with waxed linen on small core. *Courtesy of Darienne McAuley.*

'Homage to the Yuki People.' Gourd base is dyed and pyro-engraved and coiled with waxed linen on small core. *Courtesy of Darienne McAuley.*

From the Author's Collection

Green Wartyback

Egyptian

Geometric

Coiled Turquoise

Brown Wartyback

Suppliers

U.S. Suppliers

These are all the suppliers that I use frequently. There are many others that I have not mentioned, only because I haven't bought their product. This is not a reflection of the quality of their products, just the limit of my needs.

Raw Gourd Suppliers

Ghost Creek Gourds, 2108 Ghost Creek Road, Laurens, South Carolina, 29360; 864-682-5251; www.ghostcreekgourds.com.

Harry Hurley, 259 Fletcher Ave, Fuquay Varina, North Carolina 27526; 919-557-5946.

Tom Keller Gourds, P.O. Box 1115, West Point, Mississippi, 39773; 662-494-3334.

Pumpkin Hollow, 610 CR 336, Piggott, Arkansas 72454; 870-598-3568; www.pumpkinhollow.com.

Sandlady's Gourd Farm, 10295 N 700 W., Tangier, Indiana, 47952; 765-498-5428; www.sandlady.com.

Welburn Farms, 40635 De Luz Road, Fallbrook, California, 92028; 877-420-2613; www.welburngourdfarm.com.

Wuertz Farm, 2487 East Highway 287, Casa Grande, Arizona, 85294; 520-723-4432; www.wuertzfarm.com.

Gourd Tools and Materials

Arizona Gourds by Bonnie Gibson, 5930 Camino Arizpe, Tucson, Arizona, 85718; 520-299-3627; www.arizonagourds.com.

Mardi Gourds, Birmingham, Alabama, 35217; 205-841-2111; www.mardigourds.com.

Primitive Originals, 344 Creekside Drive, Leesburg, Georgia, 31763; 229-420-9982; www.primitiveoriginals.com.

Primitive Originals Too, 304 Chehaw Park Road, Albany, Georgia 31701; 229-432-7109; www.primitiveoriginalstoo.com.

Royalwood Ltd, 517 Woodville Road, Mansfield, Ohio, 44907; 800-526-1630; www.royalwoodltd.com.

The Caning Shop, 926 Gilman Street, Berkeley, California, 94710; 800-544-3373; www.caningshop.com.

Turtle Feathers, P.O. Box 1307, Bryson City, North Carolina, 28713; 828-926-4716; www.turtlefeathers.com.

Canadian Suppliers

Raw Gourd Suppliers

Northern Dipper Farms, 5376 County Road 56, RR2, Cookstown, Ontario, L0L 1L0; 705-435-3307; www.northerndipper.com.

Gourd Tools and Materials

Lee Valley Tools, www.leevalley.com.

MacPherson Arts & Crafts, 91 Queen Street, East, Box 1810, St. Mary's, Ontario, N4X 1C2; 800-238-6663; www.macphersoncrafts.com.

Northern Dipper Farms, 5376 County Road 56, RR2, Cookstown, Ontario, L0L 1L0; 705-435-3307; www.northerndipper.com.

Thompson's Woodcarving, 15 Clairmont Street, Sudbury, Ontario, P3B 3S4; 877-503-1601; www.northerncarver.com.

Bibliography

Arnoldussen, Margaret (Peg). *Coiled Art With Pine Needles and Raffia*. Self-published at http://pinebaskets.tripod.com.

Bibby, Brian. *The Fine Art of California Indian Basketry: Crocker Art Museum*. Sacramento, California: Crocker Art Museum in association with Heyday Books, 1996.

Callaghan, Margo M. *Baskets of the Wounaan and Emberá Indians from the Darién Rainforest of Panamá*. 2nd Edition, edited in Panamá. Sun Lakes, Arizona: HPL Enterprises, Revised 2004.

Chancey, Jill R. and Cook, Stephen W. *By Native Hands: Woven Treasures from the Lauren Rogers Museum of Art*. Laurel, Mississippi: Lauren Rogers Museum of Art, 2005.

McFarland, Jeannie. *Pine Needle Raffia Basketry*. Redmond Provo, Utah: Press Printing, Revised 1996.

Moore, Marilyn and Thomas, Katherine G. *Introduction to Coiling*. Xbasket: 2001-02 (CD-ROM).

Pulleyn, Rob. *The Basketmaker's Art: Contemporary Baskets and Their Makers*. Asheville, North Carolina: Lark Books, 1986.

Summit, Ginger and Widess, Jim. *The Complete Book of Gourd Craft*. Asheville, North Carolina: Lark Books, 1996.

Teiwes, Helga. *Hopi Basket Weaving: Artistry in Natural Fibers*. Tucson, Arizona: University Press, 1996.

Turnbaugh, Sarah Peabody and Turnbaugh, William A. *Indian Baskets: Revised Price Guide*. Atglen, Pennsylvania: Schiffer Publishing Ltd., 2004.

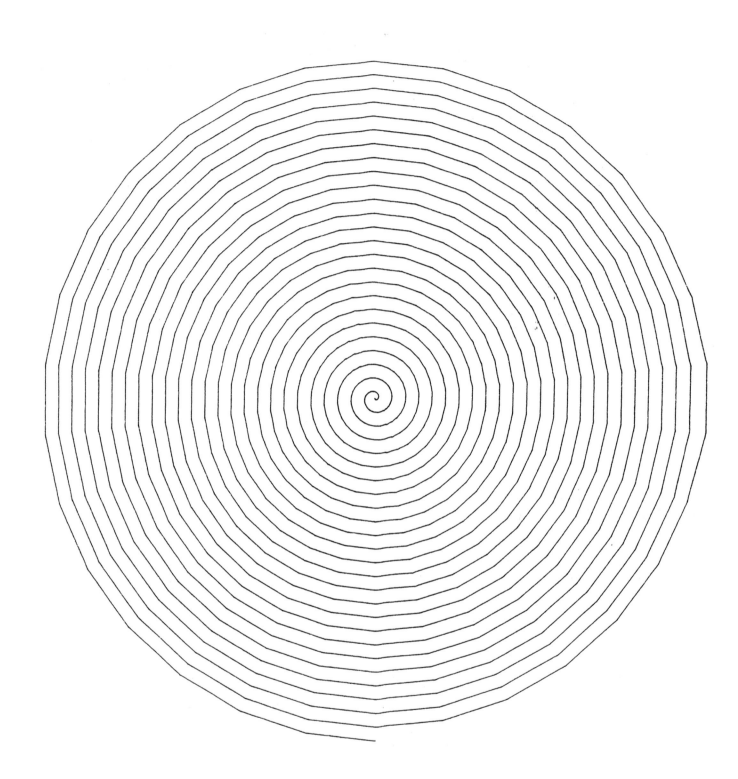